# The English Language
# Common Law Workbook

# The English Language Common Law Workbook

*A Resource for Students Studying English-Medium Law Degrees*

*Ian Collins & David Brody*

University of Michigan Press
*Ann Arbor*

Published in the United States of America by the
University of Michigan Press
Manufactured in the United States of America
Printed on acid-free paper

ISBN 978-0-472-03995-1 (print)
ISBN 978-0-472-22226-1 (e-book)

First published August 2025

# Contents

# Acknowledgments

Many people have contributed directly or indirectly to this book, but firstly, we would like to thank students at Yaşar University and the University of Houston Law Center who have worked through many iterations of some of the exercises, giving us invaluable feedback along the way.

Burcu Dönmez, dean of the Faculty of Law at Yaşar University, has strongly supported legal English at the university and given us carte blanche to design support courses however we wanted. Similarly, members of the School of Foreign Languages, especially Aylin Atacan and Dilek Arca, have provided much-needed moral support and freedom to pursue our interests outside the English for Academic Purposes program's main courses.

Karen Jones, Cheryl Zingaro, Kate Brem, and Laurel Simmons of the University of Houston Law Center have also been very helpful, both generally with input on the design of pre-sessional courses for foreign LL.M. (legum magister, or master of laws) students, and also along the way with suggestions and feedback on the project. Our experiences with the Houston LL.M. students acted as the catalyst for putting together a workbook such as this.

Katie LaPlant at the University of Michigan Press helped us to keep faith in the project and provided feedback that made the book much, much better. Her unfailing enthusiasm and professionalism are greatly appreciated.

Zehra Sak Brody enthusiastically cheered on this project from the very beginning. Without her support, it would have taken a great deal longer to get it done.

Lastly, a big fatherly thanks to İdil Collins. Her enthusiasm for working through the exercises, despite not having anything to do with the law nor being a law student, helped us realize the workbook could engage students from all over the world, whatever their background.

# Introduction

*There is no jewel in the world comparable to learning; no learning so excellent as knowledge of laws.*

> —Sir Edward Coke, 16th- and 17th-century English jurist
> and one of the fathers of modern common law.

Studying law is a challenging endeavor for everyone. Not only does it involve learning a huge amount of detail, but it also requires students to develop particular ways of speaking and writing that are often quite different from how most people use language in the everyday world. In fact, critics have frequently accused the legal profession of deliberately trying to exclude ordinary people by communicating in an arcane and overly obscure language (what they mockingly refer to as "legalese"). On top of these difficulties, all legal jurisdictions have developed their own distinctive culture, which affects every part of the system, from the language to how you even think about legal issues.

With that in mind, this workbook is designed as a tool for acculturating students of law whose first language is not English and who are not closely familiar with the common law,[1] and who are aiming to pursue their studies in English—particularly those wanting to complete LL.M. degrees in the United States, the United Kingdom, or some other English-speaking country. It may also help teachers of those students, such as those preparing pre-sessional courses for students going on to do LL.M. degrees. It may even help practitioners in civil law jurisdictions whose first language is not English but who want to do legal work in common law countries in English.

Despite these aims, this workbook is neither, strictly speaking, a law textbook, nor an English-language textbook. If you are a student, you may learn some law by doing the exercises within it. You will certainly improve your legal English skills. However, it is not focused on particular aspects of law nor use of language per se. There are very few, for example, pure grammar exercises contained within it.

The idea for the workbook came about after we, the authors, had spent many hundreds of hours designing authentic or semi-authentic materials to help our students learn some of the strategies they needed to read and write in English in a common law context. What became clear over the years was that some of the hurdles to achieving competence in English to be able to study successfully in English-medium law courses were far greater than the challenge of mastering discipline-specific terminology or learning particular grammar structures in legal texts. On top of this, many textbooks of legal English were either too simple or much too difficult for our students.

As we tried ways of getting around this problem by heavily adapting published materials, it became clear that, in order to be successful, our students needed to understand some of the concepts of common law. They also, for example, needed to get familiar with how statutes and cases in common law countries are written and structured. They needed exposure to the *discourse* of common law legal thinking and writing.[2] When expressed like this, it appears as if it could be very complex and difficult for students whose first language is not English. However, our experience is that when students are given well-designed materials and supported, they can quickly adapt themselves to new ways of thinking that greatly help them when faced with legal reading and writing tasks in English.

Therefore, this workbook aims to provide a wide range of semi-authentic and authentic materials for students to develop and practice the skills they need to be successful in endeavors such as LL.M. programs in the United States or elsewhere. We assume the students have a good, general level of English (around at least B2 on the Common European Framework of Reference for Languages scale in most areas). By completing the exercises, students will acquire not only a range of useful terminology but also strategies for reading such things as common law statutes and cases. Moreover, they will learn some basic writing techniques that they will be able to apply for the rest of their academic and professional careers as lawyers. Finally, they will have ample practice of "thinking like a common law lawyer" (those analytical skills that can appear elusive and difficult to learn). Not only will this give them a significant benefit if studying for qualifications such as an LL.M., it will help open the path for them to practice law in a common law jurisdiction.[3]

While all the materials are based around real law, the statutes and cases used have, in most instances, been edited for brevity or had multiple legal issues stripped down to a single one. This has been done deliberately so as not to overwhelm students. After all, as we have said previously, the workbook is not a legal textbook. Its overriding aim is to support students reading and writing in a legal context in a language that is not their mother tongue. Moreover, we have tried to take materials from different common law jurisdictions to provide as much breadth as possible. That said, overall, the majority come from the United States. In addition, owing to various factors (e.g., length of case; engaging quality of the subject matter etc.), criminal matters tend to predominate among the materials offered in the workbook. We acknowledge this may not suit all students. However, we are confident that any student who successfully works their way through the exercises in the workbook will be well prepared to take on different types of legal matters and use the skills they have learned in any common law jurisdiction.

How should a student use this workbook? Firstly, do not necessarily think of it as a main coursebook that you need to work through systematically in order, completing every exercise (though you may choose to do this if you want to). Depending on your experience and competence with legal English, you can dip into the exercises that you feel would be beneficial. If you are undertaking self-study, try to identify which areas you wish to improve in and choose the exercises accordingly. If you are a teacher using the workbook, you can likewise dip in and use whatever materials suit your lesson plan. You can amend the exercises yourself, or even abandon them altogether and use the statutes or cases included to design your own.

Most of the exercises have answers provided for them so you can check your work. In many cases, these are very much suggested acceptable answers. There are many other ways to complete them correctly. Hopefully, as you become more experienced doing these types of exercises, you will start to recognize that there are generally applicable approaches that support you to complete them successfully. Once you start to feel this, it is a sign that you have begun to "think like a common law lawyer," which is a big step along the way to succeeding in studying law or working in an English-speaking legal environment.

However you will use this book, it would be helpful to give you some explanation of how the chapters are organized. Each one starts with a general introduction of the overall skill being focused on (for example, reading statutes). It will highlight some of the key strategies necessary for that skill and introduce certain specific techniques or structures (for example, the basics of how to put together a case brief).

It will then list the learning outcomes for the chapter. These are statements of what you should be able to do once you have completed all the exercises. This is a useful way for you to understand what you are aiming for and also to gauge your progress.

After the introduction to each chapter, there are a number of exercises for you to work on. We have deliberately made these as diverse as possible, and there is no common thread running through the statutes and cases we have chosen. Rather, they are all used to practice the specific skills covered in the chapter. Each exercise starts with some warm-up activity or task for you to do to introduce you to the legal issue covered in that exercise. These are followed by some language exercises that will support your reading of the legal texts (statutes or cases) that form the subject of the exercise. These focus on such things as key vocabulary; specific uses of language that you may need to get familiar with or practice; or tasks that prompt you to analyze the structural components of the text. The remainder of the exercise will then focus on, for example, the actual meaning of a statute, or the legal principle established by a particular case. You may be asked to answer comprehension questions about the text or apply the law set out in the text to a hypothetical set of facts. Later on, you will also be asked to produce summaries of case law (what we call "case briefs") and written answers to legal problems following a particular structure covered in the chapter. The latter parts of each exercise require a lot of critical legal thinking.

The chapter will conclude with a reference back to the learning outcomes so that you can consider how well you have mastered each objective. As we state above, you may not need to cover every exercise, or every part of an exercise you choose to do. You or your teacher may decide to skip the earlier parts and focus on the things that are more specifically legal rather than language based. There is no right or wrong way to use these materials, it is up to you to get the most out of them. What we can confidently say is that if you can work your way through them all successfully, you will be well set up for continuing your legal studies or work in English.

At the end of the book, you will find a glossary of useful words and phrases that generally appear in the exercises or, alternatively, are important things for you to know. There is also a bibliography that does not just list materials referred to in the book but also provides references to other useful materials for further reading.

**Important note:** As mentioned above, cases (and some statutes) have been edited in various ways. Therefore, while the case citation may be authentic, the actual text may differ substantially from the real version of the case. In addition, because it does not matter in the context of the aims of the workbook, no real attempt has been made to make sure that all of the materials are still "good law." Therefore, it is important that these materials are used solely for educational purposes and not as accurate statements of law in any jurisdiction.

The American spelling of words has been adopted throughout the text. However, there are some words that are spelled differently in certain statutes and cases (most notably "defense," which is spelled "defence" in the United Kingdom). Where this occurs, the spelling in the original statute or case is preserved, but any questions about that text will adopt American English spelling.

*Chapter 1*
Reading Statutes

*Statute—a written law enacted by a legislative body*

Students sometimes imagine that in common law jurisdictions, only cases are really important. Of course, cases are fundamental in establishing the law, but common law jurisdictions in the modern era make extensive use of statutes. Large numbers of old common law cases have, in fact, been effectively overturned by later statutes. It is even quite common for, say, US states to have "codes" that appear at first glance not to be that different from the types of codes found in civil law jurisdictions. Therefore, students should not underestimate the importance of statutes in common law systems. In this chapter, we will look at some of the reading strategies that students can employ in order to successfully unpack the various provisions in statutes. There then follows a number of exercises in which you can practice these techniques and approaches with extracts from real-life statutes. In the subsequent chapters, we will see how cases link with statutes to form the body of common law.

Understanding statutes, in essence, boils down to careful reading. Therefore, any student who wants to understand the law set out in a statute cannot avoid the simple fact that that they are going to have to read it more closely than they may read other texts, such as novels or text messages. In an ideal world, a statute will not include any single unnecessary word. That means that every single one is important! As we will see, even those small words that our eyes might pass over quickly in other texts, such as "and" and "or," need to be taken into account as they will, quite literally, completely change an interpretation of the meaning of the law.

There are a number of approaches to the interpretation of statutes, sometimes referred to as protocols or "canons" of construction.[1] As you progress in your legal studies, you may find yourself studying these in detail. Some of them include investigating what the legislative body may have intended when drafting a particular statute, or looking at the relevant context to try to determine its purpose. However, these are not the focus of this chapter, which is designed to provide practice in simply navigating around the sometimes-complex structures of statutes and applying what is described in the texts when answering questions or responding to hypothetical scenarios.

However, before moving on to the exercises, it would be a good idea to think about some strategies that may assist you in unpacking the legal effect of different statutes. Firstly, modern statutes are invariably organized into numbered clauses, which may themselves be arranged into different parts. Very often, these parts have their own subheadings to assist in locating relevant clauses. At the risk of stating the obvious, often the first thing to do when reading a statute is to consider how it has been divided up into different parts and clauses, taking into account subheadings and other clues that may provide helpful information. This is likely to make it much easier to find the law that is most applicable to the context of the question you are answering.

Leading on from this, the sentence structure of statutes is often very different from how English is written in other types of documents, such as novels or web articles.[2] For example, it is very common for the main clause or main verb of a sentence to appear after subsidiary clauses, which can make it hard on a first read to understand the key point. See the following example:

1.  *Marriage out of State to evade law. When residents of this State, with intent to evade this section and to return and reside here, go into another state or country to have their marriage solemnized there and afterwards return and reside here, that marriage is void in this State.*

In order to understand the provisions of this clause from a statute, it is necessary to first read the whole thing to understand that it is setting out the conditions under which a marriage may not be valid. However, a reader will almost certainly then need to go back once, or even twice, to unpack the different elements necessary for that particular law to apply.

Moreover, as well as the sentence structure being very different, it is often necessary to refer to other parts of the statute since the clause you are reading is modified or controlled by them. This greatly adds to the complexity of what you are trying to understand. Read the following example:

*(2) Subject to subsection (3), if any person contravenes subsection (1) in respect of a place, each manager, owner and lessee of the place is deemed to have contravened that subsection . . .*

In the above clause, a reader needs to read right to the end of the sentence before the main verb is clear. In addition, there are cross-references to other subsections that impact on the meaning of subsection (2). In other words, it will be hard on a first reading to understand the provisions set out in this clause. You will probably have to read it and the other subsections referred to again, and again, and maybe even again, before it is clear.

Most statutes will also have terms that are defined for the purposes of the statute. This is almost certainly going to change the meaning from what that word or phrase may mean in general, everyday English into something much more specific for the purposes of the statute. For example, in Alaska, burglary is defined under Alaska Stat. § 11.46.310(a) (2020) and refers to the entry of a "building." In general English, people would generally understand what you meant if you used that word. However, Alaska Stat. § 11.81.900(b)(5) (2021) provides a very specific definition that may extend the meaning of that word for the purposes of the burglary statute:

*" 'Building,' in addition to its usual meaning, includes any propelled vehicle or structure adapted for overnight accommodation of persons or for carrying on business."*

When reading its provisions, you need to bear in mind that any reference to a building is to a strictly defined legal entity.

In addition to needing to take into account defined terms, you may also need to cope with words that may be unclear or ambiguous. In fact, there are a number of terms that you see in the statutes of many common law jurisdictions that are not necessarily capable of being clearly defined. For example, in the UK Defamation Act, 2013, section 2(1) states:

*It is a defence to an action for defamation for the defendant to show that the imputation conveyed by the statement complained of is substantially true.*

The meaning of "substantially" is not given in the Act. It may, in fact, require a decision to be made in a legal case for there to be some sort of clarification of what "substantially" might mean in different contexts (see the following chapter on case law). There are many other words that are clearly open to interpretation that you come across in statutes from all common law jurisdictions, such as "reasonable," "serious," or "material." When reading a statute, you may need to make a note of such ambiguities, both to factor into any answer you may be giving relating to the statute, and to search for cases that may give some guidance on how that part of the statute should be interpreted.

Finally, there are many common words that tend to be repeatedly used in statutes, and it is a good idea to try to get a firm grasp on what they mean as soon as possible. For example:

- The word *shall* is very often used to indicate an obligation (which is a little different from how it is often used in general, everyday English).
- As noted above, pay particular attention to the use of *and* and *or*, since they can often be of critical importance when interpreting the exact meaning of a statute.
- *Subject to* is used frequently to show that a particular clause is limited by another provision, often cross-referred to in the text.
- Be careful about various classes of things being limited as either included or excluded by the use of *each*, *only*, or *all* and other similar words or phrases.
- Also pay special attention to words such as *if*, *provided that*, or *in the event that*, since they refer to some sort of pre-condition required for that particular provision to have effect.

In conclusion, as is noted above, meticulous, close reading is required when trying to understand and interpret any statute, even ones that may appear at first glance to be relatively simple. It is a truism of all law and legal study that words matter, and this dictum is never more important than when reading a statute. The exercises that follow are designed to give you an opportunity to work your way through some statutory wording, applying some of the strategies that are outlined above. There are a variety of different tasks, but all require critical engagement with the text and the ability to gain a deep understanding of what is written.

By the end of the chapter, you will hopefully be able to do the following:

- Analyze the organization of statutes, including sections, subsections, and headings.
- Identify the purpose and structure of different parts within a statute.
- Identify and interpret cross-references within statutes.

- Extract the main legal principles and obligations from a given statute.
- Recognize and comprehend specialized legal terminology commonly used in common law statutes.
- Differentiate between mandatory and permissive language within statutory provisions.
- Articulate the purpose and effect of specific statutory provisions.
- Apply the provisions of a statute to the facts of a hypothetical situation to solve a legal problem.

**Note:** the exercises that follow are from or are based on real statutes. However, they have sometimes been modified for the purposes of designing the exercises. Where extensive modifications have been made, they are noted as being from fictional jurisdictions.

## Exercise 1    Serving alcohol (United States)

### Lead-in

1. Why do authorities pass laws that regulate the serving of alcohol?
2. Think about a jurisdiction that you are familiar with. What laws are there that relate to the selling and consumption of alcohol?
3. What could be some of the problems caused by not regulating the serving of alcohol, particularly to young people?

### Exercises

Read the following statutes from the fictional jurisdiction of Collody and answer the questions that follow.[3]

*Collody Civil Code section 3630:*
A person who is injured as a result of the negligent service of alcoholic beverages by a licensed alcoholic beverage server may recover damages from that server only if:

(a)  the server either served a visibly intoxicated person; or
(b)  served someone under the age of 21, under circumstances where the server knew, or reasonably should have known, that the person served was under 21; and
(c)  the injury was a foreseeable result of the negligent service of alcoholic beverages.

. . .

*Collody Civil Code section 3629:*
A licensed alcoholic beverage server may not serve alcoholic beverages to any person unless they first show legal identification proving that they are at least 21 years old.

*Collody Civil Code section 3625:*
For the purposes of section 3630, "licensed alcoholic beverage server" means a person who has been trained and licensed by this state to serve alcohol in a restaurant or bar.

## Analysis of the statute

**Choose the best answer:**

1. What is the meaning of "negligent" in section 3630?
    a. Mistakenly assuming an individual is over the age of 21.
    b. The consumption of too much alcohol without taking sufficient care about the consequences.
    c. The reckless or careless serving of alcohol to a person.
    d. Selling the wrong type of alcohol to a customer.
2. "Damages" in the statute refers to:
    a. Physical harm suffered by the person served.
    b. A court punishment imposed on the licensed alcoholic beverage server.
    c. Financial compensation that an injured party can recover.
    d. Harm suffered by the injured party.
3. "Visibly intoxicated" in section 3630(a) means:
    a. Showing clear signs of having consumed too much alcohol.
    b. Openly consuming alcohol in a public place.
    c. Consuming alcohol in a private establishment.
    d. Appearing to be ill in a place where alcohol is being served.
4. "Foreseeable" in section 3630(c) means:
    a. Injuries that resulted from serving minors under 21 without legal identification.
    b. An injury that a reasonable person could have anticipated as a consequence of negligent alcohol service.
    c. Any injury that occurs as a result of serving alcohol.
    d. Injuries that the server knew would occur if they sold alcohol to a minor.

**Answer the following questions:**

1.   What is the purpose of section 3625 of the statute?
2.   Would a person claiming damages for negligent service of alcoholic beverages have to show that every part of section 3630(a) through (c) can be established? What language and/or punctuation in the statute helps you to understand this?
3.   How does section 3629 relate to section 3630(b)?


## Application of the statute to hypothetical facts

**Answer the following questions, using appropriate sections from the statutes:**

1.   While riding his bike home from a bar where he had been drinking, Bob crashed into Mike and broke Mike's arm. The police determined that Bob was legally drunk at the time of the accident. Bob is 20 years old, but most people say he looks a year or two older. The bartender who served Bob did not ask him to show any identification before she served him. Witnesses testified that Bob did not seem drunk when he left the bar. Based only on this information, can Mike recover damages from the server under these statutes?
2.   Laura is 20 years old. While eating dinner at a restaurant with her friends, she ordered a cocktail. The waiter who served Laura did not ask her to show any identification before he served her. Unfortunately, she had a very serious allergic reaction to the mango juice in the cocktail and almost died. Based only on this information, will Laura and her family be able to recover damages from the server under these statutes?


## Exercise 2    Consumer rights (United Kingdom)

### Lead-in

**Read the text below and answer the questions:**

Jane recently purchased a brand-new smartphone from a reputable electronics shop. Excited about her purchase, she eagerly unboxed the device only to discover the camera did not seem to take good-quality photos and that there were frequent software crashes. She decided to wait a few days to see if the phone worked better, hoping it just needed to download some updates. However, on the third day, it was clear that the phone had a problem. Frustrated, Jane contacted the shop's customer services department to address the issue. However, the store initially seemed hesitant to provide a solution. They claimed that it was common for all phone software to crash from time to time and that the camera issue was down to her taking bad photos. They also pointed out their terms and conditions for a full refund for smartphones, which specified that goods had to be returned within 48 hours of purchase.

1. Since the phone worked to some extent, do you think Jane has any rights to claim a refund?
2. Many businesses have terms and conditions that regulate in what circumstances you can get a refund for a purchase you have made. Do you think they have the right to draft these terms and conditions in any way they like? Why or why not?
3. What do you think is meant by the terms "satisfactory quality" and "fit for purpose"?

## Exercises

Read these extracts from the United Kingdom Consumer Rights Act 2015[4] and answer the questions that follow.

*Part 1*

Chapter 2

**3 Contracts covered by this Chapter**
(1) This Chapter applies to a contract for a trader to supply goods to a consumer.
(2) It applies only if the contract is one of these (defined for the purposes of this Part in sections 5 to 8)—
    (a) a sales contract;
    (b) a contract for the hire of goods;
    (c) a hire-purchase agreement;
    (d) a contract for transfer of goods.

. . .

**9 Goods to be of satisfactory quality**
(1) Every contract to supply goods is to be treated as including a term that the quality of the goods is satisfactory.
(2) The quality of goods is satisfactory if they meet the standard that a reasonable person would consider satisfactory, taking account of—
    (a) any description of the goods,
    (b) the price or other consideration for the goods (if relevant), and
    (c) all the other relevant circumstances (see subsection (5)).

(3) The quality of goods includes their state and condition; and the following aspects (among others) are in appropriate cases aspects of the quality of goods—

    (a) fitness for all the purposes for which goods of that kind are usually supplied;

    (b) appearance and finish;

    (c) freedom from minor defects;

    (d) safety;

    (e) durability.

(4) The term mentioned in subsection (1) does not cover anything which makes the quality of the goods unsatisfactory—

    (a) which is specifically drawn to the consumer's attention before the contract is made,

    (b) where the consumer examines the goods before the contract is made, which that examination ought to reveal, or

    (c) in the case of a contract to supply goods by sample, which would have been apparent on a reasonable examination of the sample.

(5) The relevant circumstances mentioned in subsection (2)(c) include any public statement about the specific characteristics of the goods made by the trader, the producer or any representative of the trader or the producer.

(6) That includes, in particular, any public statement made in advertising or labelling.


## Relevant definitions

"Consumer" means an individual acting for purposes that are wholly or mainly outside that individual's trade, business, craft or profession.


## Analysis of the statute

1. Section 3(1) of the statute notes that the section applies to a contract for a trader to supply goods to a consumer. What is a "consumer" for the purposes of the statute?

2. The statute only covers certain types of contracts. Where do we find which contracts are included?

3. What is the effect of section 9(1)?

4. Section 9(2) lists things that need to be taken into account when assessing whether the quality of a good supplied is satisfactory. How does the

statute make it clear that all factors listed as (a), (b), and (c) should be included?

5. Section 9(4) lists some circumstances in which section 9(1) will not apply to a contract. Do you need to show every circumstance listed in (a) through (c) or just one of them? How does the statute show this?

**Mark the following statements as True (T) or False (F):**

1. This statute would imply a term that the quality of goods supplied was satisfactory if the contract was between two companies. **T / F**
2. A contract to provide IT consultancy services by a firm to an individual would not be covered by this statute. **T / F**
3. The price of the goods supplied can be a relevant factor in determining whether their quality is satisfactory. **T / F**
4. The satisfactory quality term would be implied even if the buyer knew about a defect before they bought it. **T / F**
5. Anything stated about the product in an advertisement can be relevant in assessing whether the goods are of satisfactory quality. **T / F**

**Answer the following questions:**

1. One factor in assessing quality is how long a product lasts (durability—9(3)(c)). What impact might this have on your rights under the statute if you bought a cheap kettle that broke after 24 months compared to a very expensive premium one that broke after 36 months?
2. Imagine that you pick up a leather jacket in a store and notice a very small mark on the collar. You buy it anyway because you like it and it is the last one in stock. Three months later, the mark increases in size and you want to return it. Does the statute help you?
3. You see an online advertisement for a cheap laptop. The advertisement shows a picture of someone using that model to play your favorite online game. You buy the laptop but when you try to play the game, you realize the laptop does not have the minimum specifications to run it properly. What arguments are available to you under the statute?

## Exercise 3   Selling tobacco and vaping products (Canada)

### Lead-in

1. Why have electronic cigarettes (vapes) become a controversial topic?
2. Do you think restricting the sale of such things as cigarettes and vapes to young people is effective in tackling addiction and unhealthy lifestyles?

Exercises

Read these extracts from the British Columbia, Canada, Tobacco And Vapour Products Control Act [RSBC 1996] Chapter 451[5] and answer the questions that follow.

*2.1 Tobacco and vapour products not to be sold in certain places*
(1) A person must not deal in, sell, offer for sale or distribute tobacco or vapour products in any of the following places:
  (a) ...
  (b) the campus of a public university or other public post-secondary institution;
  (c) a building or structure that is owned or leased by a public body that is used primarily for athletic or recreation purposes;

     . . .

(2) Subject to subsection (3), if any person contravenes subsection (1) in respect of a place, each manager, owner and lessee of the place is deemed to have contravened that subsection and each is liable for the contravention.
(3) It is a defence to a charge under subsection (2) if the manager, owner or lessee, as applicable, demonstrates that he or she exercised reasonable care and diligence to prevent the contravention.
(4) Subsection (2) applies whether or not the person who dealt in, sold, offered for sale or distributed tobacco or vapour products, or any other person, is charged with contravening subsection (1).

*3 Enforcement officers*
(1) The minister may designate as enforcement officers any persons or categories of persons the minister considers qualified to be so designated.
(2) To carry out the duties of an enforcement officer under this Act, an enforcement officer may at any reasonable time enter and inspect any place
  (a) to which the public has access and where tobacco or vapour products are offered for sale, or
  (b) to which any of sections 2.1 to 2.3 apply.

     . . .

(4) A person must not
  (a) hinder, obstruct or otherwise interfere with an enforcement officer who is acting under this Act, or
  (b) knowingly make a false or misleading statement, or provide or produce a false document or thing, to an enforcement officer who is acting under this Act.

## Analysis of the statute

**Match the following words with the correct definition:**

| Word or phrase | Definition |
| --- | --- |
| 1. deal in | a. to violate or breach a law or regulation |
| 2. distribute | b. to officially assign or appoint someone to a particular role or position |
| 3. lease | c. to be considered or regarded as |
| 4. contravene | d. to engage in the buying and selling of goods, services, or property |
| 5. deemed to | e. to provide something, such as information or goods, to multiple recipients |
| 6. reasonable care and diligence | f. to rent or let someone use a property for a specified period in exchange for payment |
| 7. designate | g. the level of caution, attention, and prudence that a sensible person would exercise under similar circumstances |

**Mark the following statements as True (T) or False (F):**

1. Pursuant to section 2.1(1), the sale of vapes would be banned in all the places listed in 2.1(1)(a) through (c). **T / F**
2. If the manager of a café is liable under section 2.1(2), the owner cannot be held liable for the same thing. **T / F**
3. The words "subject to subsection (3)" means that section 2.1(2) will apply to a charge under section 2.1(1) unless there is a defense available. **T / F**
4. An enforcement officer may enter any private area at any time to inspect a premises they suspect of selling tobacco or vapor products. **T / F**

**Consider the situation outlined below:**

Brad is the owner of a coffee shop called Brain Juice. It is located in a bookstore on a public community college campus in British Columbia, Canada. Brain Juice leases the space from the bookstore. Although Brad owns Brain Juice, he has another full-time job and seldom comes in. Instead, he leaves the day-to-day management to Dawn, his trusted manager.

Dory is a representative of an e-cigarette company. Dory visited the shop and spoke to Dawn about placing a small display with their products near the cash register. Dawn decided to sign a one-year contract with Dory's company.

After Brain Juice had been selling the e-cigarettes for several weeks, an enforcement officer called Brad and asked him to come to the shop. She asked

Brad why he was selling these products in violation of the law. Brad replied, truthfully, that he had no idea that Brain Juice was selling e-cigarettes. He also said that he had specifically told Dawn not to sell any tobacco or vaping products at the shop. This was not true.

**Multiple choice—choose the best answer:**

1.  Which of the following individuals is probably not guilty of violating section 2.1?
    a.  Brad
    b.  Dory
    c.  Dawn
    d.  none of the above
2.  Which of the following best expresses why Brad is guilty of violating section 2.1?
    a.  Brad is guilty of violating section 2.1(1)(b) because he told the enforcement officer a lie.
    b.  Dory and Dawn violated 2.1(1)(b) by distributing and selling e-cigarettes at a shop on a college campus, so Brad is guilty as the shop owner under section 2.1(2).
    c.  Brad is guilty of violating 2.1(3), which requires the owner of a coffee shop on a college campus to diligently prevent the sale of e-cigarettes.
    d.  Answers b. and c. are both true.
3.  Assume that Dawn is not charged with violating section 2.1. Can Brad still be charged with violating it?
    a.  Yes, because according to section 2.1(4) he can still be charged under section 2.1(2).
    b.  Yes, because he had several weeks to find out that Brain Juice was selling e-cigarettes.
    c.  No, because Brad left the day-to-day management of Brain Juice to Dawn.
    d.  No, because the coffee shop is used primarily for recreation purposes as permitted by 2.1(2)(c).

**Answer the following questions:**

1.  Has anyone violated section 3(4)(a) or (b)?
2.  Other than Dory, Dawn, and Brad, are there any people or entities that might be guilty of violating section 2.1?
3.  Do Dory, Dawn, Brad, or any of the other possible people or entities that you think might be guilty of violating section 2.1 have any potential defenses?

4.  Assume that all the facts are as stated above, but that Brad really had told Dawn not to sell any vaping products. How would Brad's potential criminal liability be different in this situation?

## Exercise 4    Child abduction (United Kingdom)

### Lead-in

Child abduction is a distressing and surprisingly widespread issue. While abductions by strangers garner significant attention, the reality is that, in many cases, family members perpetrate these crimes. This adds a complex layer to the problem. Family abductions may arise from custody disputes, strained relationships, or even a misguided belief that the abductor is acting in the child's best interest. The serious consequences of familial abductions underscore the need for preventive measures, effective legal frameworks, and support systems to safeguard children from harm and ensure their well-being. From a legal perspective in the United Kingdom, the Child Abduction Act 1984 provides a comprehensive approach to dealing with situations where a child is wrongfully removed from the country and taken abroad. The key rationale is to protect the welfare and best interests of the child.

1.  What do you understand by the word "abduction"?
2.  Why do you think the abduction of a child by a family member is legally often more complicated than if done by a stranger?

### Exercises

Read these extracts from the United Kingdom Child Abduction Act 1984[6] and answer the questions that follow.

*Part I*

1 Offence of abduction of child by parent, etc.
(1)  Subject to subsection (5) [and (8)] below, a person connected with a child under the age of sixteen commits an offence if he takes or sends the child out of the United Kingdom without the appropriate consent.
(2)  A person is connected with a child for the purposes of this section if—
    (a)  he is a parent of the child; or
    (b)  in the case of a child whose parents were not married to, or civil partners of, each other at the time of his birth, there are reasonable grounds for believing that he is the father of the child; or

    (c)  he is a guardian of the child; or

    (ca) he is a special guardian of the child; or

    (d)  he is a person named in a child arrangements order as a person with whom the child is to live; or

    (e)  he has custody of the child.

(3)  In this section 'the appropriate consent', in relation to a child, means—

    (a)  the consent of each of the following—

        (i)     the child's mother;

        (ii)    the child's father, if he has parental responsibility for him;

        (iii)   any guardian of the child;

        (iiia) any special guardian of the child;

        (iv)   any person named in a child arrangements order as a person with whom the child is to live;

        (iv)   any person who has custody of the child; or

    (b)  the leave of the court granted under or by virtue of any provision of Part II of the Children Act 1989; or

    (c)  if any person has custody of the child, the leave of the court which awarded custody to him.

. . .

(5)  A person does not commit an offence under this section by doing anything without the consent of another person whose consent is required under the foregoing provisions if—

    (a)  he does it in the belief that the other person—

        (i)   has consented; or

        (ii)  would consent if he was aware of all the relevant circumstances; or

    (b)  he has taken all reasonable steps to communicate with the other person but has been unable to communicate with him; or

    (c)  the other person has unreasonably refused to consent.

## Analysis of the statute

**Complete the sentences using the words from the box.**

| provisions | parental responsibility | custody | guardian |
|---|---|---|---|

1.  The _______________ of the young orphan was appointed after the tragic incident, ensuring there was someone responsible to care for the child's well-being.

2. ________________ refers to the legal rights, duties, and authority a parent has in making decisions about a child's upbringing, including matters related to education, healthcare, and religion. It emphasizes the responsibilities and obligations of parents toward their children. On the other hand, ________________ typically refers to the physical care and control of a child.

3. The lawyer reviewed all the ________________ of the contract, in order to be able to explain to her client all their rights and responsibilities under the agreement.

**Answer the following questions:**

1. Under section 1 (2) of the Act, would someone need to show they came within all subsections (a) through (e) to be said to be "connected" to a child? What language in the statute shows this?

2. If someone wanted to demonstrate they had obtained consent under section 1 (3)(a), would they have to have obtained consent from each of the persons listed (where relevant)? What language in the statute shows this?

3. What do you think is "reasonable" for the purposes of section 1 (5)(b)? Can you think of any particular circumstances that may be relevant in deciding whether it was reasonable?

**Mark the following statements as True (T) or False (F):**

1. It is an offense under section 1(1) of the Act for a person connected to a child under the age of 18 to take that child out of the United Kingdom without the appropriate consent. **T / F**

2. You are a "person connected with a child" under the Act if you are their parent, or guardian, or have custody of them. **T / F**

3. To obtain "appropriate consent" under the Act, the consent of all the people listed in section (3)(a), if relevant, is required. **T / F**

4. Appropriate consent can be withheld under any circumstances. **T / F**

5. No offense under the Act would be committed if a person connected with a child took the child out of the United Kingdom believing that they had the required appropriate consent to do so. **T / F**

**Complete the following sentences with the best option.**

1. A child's father may have the right to give "appropriate consent" if ____
   ________________________________.
   a. he is the child's biological father
   b. he is the sole guardian of the child

    c.  the mother has given consent

    d.  he has parental responsibility for the child

2.  It would <u>not</u> be an offense under the Act if _______________________.

    a.  appropriate consent was reasonably withheld from the person taking a child out of the United Kingdom but they decided to take the child anyway

    b.  the person taking the child out of the United Kingdom believed there were circumstances that meant appropriate consent would be given

    c.  the person taking the child out of the United Kingdom without consent was well known to the child

    d.  if the child wanted the person to take them out of the United Kingdom even though that person had not obtained the appropriate consent

3.  A divorced husband with no parental responsibilities over a child would <u>not</u> commit an offense under the Act if, before he took his child out of the United Kingdom, he ________________________________.

    a.  sent a WhatsApp message and email to his ex-wife in good time to obtain appropriate consent but no response was received

    b.  telephoned his ex-wife once but left no message when she did not pick up the call

    c.  informed the child's school about the plan

    d.  informed the child's grandparents

## Exercise 5    Kidnapping (United States)[7]

### Lead-in

1.  Kidnapping is a fairly common theme in movies and television thrillers. What elements does it usually involve? What are fictional kidnappers usually trying to achieve?

2.  What factors should lawmakers take into account when deciding which kidnappings to punish most severely?

3.  You will notice that in the statutes below, both Washington and Oregon exclude a common reason for taking a person somewhere against their will. What is that situation? Do you agree with their choice?

Read these extracts from the statutes of two American states. Then, complete the vocabulary exercise. Finally, decide if anyone might be guilty of violating either of the statutes in the hypothetical situations that follow.

## Washington

*RCW 9A.40.020 Kidnapping in the first degree.*
(1) A person is guilty of kidnapping in the first degree if he or she intentionally abducts another person with intent:
    (a) To hold him or her for ransom or reward, or as a shield or hostage; or
    (b) To facilitate commission of any felony or flight thereafter; or
    (c) To inflict bodily injury on him or her; or
    (d) To inflict extreme mental distress on him, her, or a third person; or
    (e) To interfere with the performance of any governmental function.

*RCW 9A.40.030 Kidnapping in the second degree.*
(1) A person is guilty of kidnapping in the second degree if he or she intentionally abducts another person under circumstances not amounting to kidnapping in the first degree.
(2) In any prosecution for kidnapping in the second degree, it is a defense if established by the defendant by a preponderance of the evidence that (a) the abduction does not include the use of or intent to use or threat to use deadly force, and (b) the actor is a relative of the person abducted, and (c) the actor's sole intent is to assume custody of that person. Nothing contained in this paragraph shall constitute a defense to a prosecution for, or preclude a conviction of, any other crime.

## Oregon

*ORS 163.235 Kidnapping in the first degree.*
(1) A person commits the crime of kidnapping in the first degree if the person violates ORS 163.225 (Kidnapping in the second degree) with any of the following purposes:
    (a) To compel any person to pay or deliver money or property as ransom;
    (b) To hold the victim as a shield or hostage;
    (c) To cause physical injury to the victim;
    (d) To terrorize the victim or another person;

. . .

*ORS 163.225 Kidnapping in the second degree.*

(1)  A person commits the crime of kidnapping in the second degree if, with intent to interfere substantially with another's personal liberty, and without consent or legal authority, the person:
  (a)  Takes the person from one place to another; or
  (b)  Secretly confines the person in a place where the person is not likely to be found.
(2)  It is a defense to a prosecution under subsection (1) of this section if:
  (a)  The person taken or confined is under 16 years of age;
  (b)  The defendant is a relative of that person; and
  (c)  The sole purpose of the person is to assume control of that person.

## Analysis of the statutes

**Read the text and fill in the blanks with words from the box.**

| | | | | |
|---|---|---|---|---|
| flight | compel | hostage | inflict | abducted |
| ransom | confined | felony | reward | constitutes |

Sean Hills picked up the phone: "We've _______ your daughter!" said a voice on the other end of the line. "If you don't pay us a _______ of $1,000,000, you will never see her again!" Hills replied, "You can't _______ me to pay that money—I'm going to get her back, myself! In fact, I'll bring you all to justice and you'll pay dearly for your crimes—what you've done _______ kidnapping, which is a major _______ in this state!"

Hills tracked the kidnappers down to an abandoned warehouse. He learned that his daughter was _______ with several others in a small room in the back. "I know you guys are in there!" Hills shouted, "Let everyone go or I'll _______ punishment on you myself!" Thinking that they must be surrounded, the kidnappers panicked. "You'd better let us get to the airport!" they shouted, "In fact, we're taking your daughter with us as a _______, to make sure you don't interfere."

However, before they could begin their _______, Hills burst into the warehouse, captured the kidnappers and freed everyone. (It helped that the kidnappers were all terrible shots.) After everyone was safe, the families of the other rescued victims were so grateful, they offered Hills a _______, which he, of course, refused.

## Application of the statute to facts

1.  Two men hold up a clothing store. The first man points a gun at the cashier and demands all of the money in the register. He tells the cashier that he will let him go as soon as he is sure that he can get away before the police show up and "won't need anyone to walk out of the store with us." The second man circulates through the store, demanding that the customers hand over their money and valuables. Both men then march everyone in the store, at gunpoint, to a storeroom in the back. They lock the door. The police arrive and release them a few minutes later.

2.  A woman works at an amusement park as a janitor. Her supervisor knows that she has a severe developmental disability. One day, the supervisor tells her to get into his car, taking care to make sure that nobody sees this. The supervisor drives them to his cabin in the woods, 10 miles from town. The supervisor tells the janitor that her new job is to take care of his elderly mother, who lives there. He also tells her that she will be paid twice what she was earning at the park, and that this would be deposited directly into an account for her. In fact, there is no account, and all that the supervisor provides for the janitor is some simple food and a small room to live in.

3.  A bookkeeper is going through the books of a business. He finds evidence that someone has been underreporting its earnings to state and federal tax officials for several years. The accountant tells one of the executives about this. Unbeknownst to the bookkeeper, she is the person most responsible for the irregularities. The executive tells the bookkeeper that, due to his excellent work, she has chosen him to accompany her on a "working vacation" aboard her yacht. She keeps him at sea for a week. Meanwhile, she directs one of her assistants to dispose of the evidence of her wrongdoing before they return.

4.  A couple are divorced and the mother has primary custody of their 15-year-old daughter. After the mother remarries, she converts to the religion of her new husband and they enroll the child in a school connected with this religion. The child's father strongly objects to his daughter attending the school; however, a court holds that the mother can make this decision. Soon after this ruling, the father picks his daughter up from school so that she can spend the weekend with him, in accordance with his visitation rights. However, rather than bring her back after the end of her visit, the father drives her to another state and enrolls the daughter, under a false name, in a school connected with his own religion.

## Exercise 6    Identity theft (Australia)

### Lead-in

**Consider the following situation:**

Using your housemate's passport, you manage to open a credit card account with an online bank. You then spend thousands of dollars buying electronics and flights. When he eventually discovers what you have done, you explain it by saying you always intended to pay the money back and that you only did it because your credit score was insufficient for you to apply for a credit card in your own name.

1.  Do you think it is possible any crime might have been committed in this scenario? Why or why not?
2.  Most countries now have laws to deal with crimes committed using technology such as the internet, etc. Why was it necessary to develop these laws when there were already criminal offenses relating to stealing and fraud in existence?
3.  What do you understand by the term "identity theft"? Why is it a potentially serious crime?

### Exercises

Read this extract from the state of New South Wales, Australia Crimes Act 1900 No 40[8] relating to identity theft and answer the questions that follow.

### Part 4AB

*Part 4AB Identity offences*

192I Definitions
In this Part—
***deal*** in identification information includes make, supply or use any such information.

    ***identification information*** means information relating to a person (whether living or dead, real or fictitious, or an individual or body corporate) that is capable of being used (whether alone or in conjunction with other information) to identify or purportedly identify the person, and includes the following—

(a) a name or address,
(b) a date or place of birth, marital status, relative's identity or similar information,
(c) a driver licence or driver licence number,

(d)  a passport or passport number,

(e)  biometric data,

(f)  a voice print,

(g)  a credit or debit card, its number or data stored or encrypted on it,

(h)  a financial account number, user name or password,

(i)  a digital signature,

(j)  a series of numbers or letters (or both) intended for use as a means of personal identification,

(k)  an ABN.

### 192J Dealing with identification information

A person who deals in identification information with the intention of committing, or of facilitating the commission of, an indictable offence* is guilty of an offence.

### 192K Possession of identification information

A person who possesses identification information with the intention of committing, or of facilitating the commission of, an indictable offence is guilty of an offence.

### 192L Possession of equipment etc to make identification documents or things

A person who—

(a)  possesses any equipment, material or other thing that is capable of being used to make a document or other thing containing identification information, and

(b)  intends that the document or other thing made will be used to commit, or to facilitate the commission of, an indictable offence, is guilty of an offence.

### 192M Miscellaneous provisions

(1)  This Part does not apply to dealing in a person's own identification information.

. . .

## Analysis of the statute

**Mark the following statements as True (T) or False (F):**

1.  The definition of "deal in identification" under the Act includes giving identification information to a third party. **T / F**

---

* similar to a felony under US law

2. Identification information under the Act must relate to a person who is alive. **T / F**
3. Identification information would include information about a company that made it possible to identify the name of that company. **T / F**
4. Only the information listed in section 192I (a) through (k) can be treated as identification information for the purposes of the Act. **T / F**

**Answer the following questions:**

1. Someone gives you their bank card to withdraw money for them from an ATM. Since you would be dealing in identification information relating to another person (i.e., using their credit card), have you committed an offense under Part 4AB?
2. You and your roommate share a laptop for surfing the internet and checking emails. He has shared his Amazon login details with you so you can check the prices of things from time to time. When logged in one time, you notice a great deal on Amazon for an iPhone. You order it using his login and bank information, knowing that you don't have the money to pay him back. Would you be guilty of an offense under Part 4AB of the Act?
3. Fred, who is 16 years old, electronically scans his own identity card with the intention of creating a fake ID to drink alcohol. Can he be guilty of an offense under Part 4AB of the Act?

## Exercise 7    Air rage (Canada)

Read this extract from the Criminal Code of Canada[9] relating to crimes committed on airplanes and answer the questions that follow.

### Lead-in

1. What does "air rage" mean? What are some of the reasons for it?
2. What tools do the flight crew have to deal with passengers who may pose a danger to other passengers, or to the flight itself?

*Use of force on board an aircraft*
**27.1 (1)** Every person on an aircraft in flight is justified in using as much force as is reasonably necessary to prevent the commission of an offence against this Act or another Act of Parliament that the person believes on reasonable grounds, if it were committed, would be likely to cause immediate and serious injury to the aircraft or to any person or property therein.

*Application of this section*
**(2)** This section applies in respect of any aircraft in flight in Canadian airspace and in respect of any aircraft registered in Canada in accordance with the regulations made under the Aeronautics Act in flight outside Canadian airspace.

. . .

*Hijacking*
**76** Every one who, unlawfully, by force or threat thereof, or by any other form of intimidation, seizes or exercises control of an aircraft with intent

a)   to cause any person on board the aircraft to be confined or imprisoned against his will,
b)   to cause any person on board the aircraft to be transported against his will to any place other than the next scheduled place of landing of the aircraft,
c)   to hold any person on board the aircraft for ransom or to service against his will, or
d)   to cause the aircraft to deviate in a material respect from its flight plan,

is guilty of an indictable offence and liable to imprisonment for life. 1972, c. 13, s. 6.

*Endangering safety of aircraft or airport*
**77** Every one who

a)   on board an aircraft in flight, commits an act of violence against a person that is likely to endanger the safety of the aircraft,
b)   using a weapon, commits an act of violence against a person at an airport serving international civil aviation that causes or is likely to cause serious injury or death and that endangers or is likely to endanger safety at the airport,
c)   causes damage to an aircraft in service that renders the aircraft incapable of flight or that is likely to endanger the safety of the aircraft in flight,
d)   places or causes to be placed on board an aircraft in service anything that is likely to cause damage to the aircraft, that will render it incapable of flight or that is likely to endanger the safety of the aircraft in flight,
e)   causes damage to or interferes with the operation of any air navigation facility where the damage or interference is likely to endanger the safety of an aircraft in flight,
f)   using a weapon, substance or device, destroys or causes serious damage to the facilities of an airport serving international civil aviation or to any aircraft not in service located there, or causes disruption of services of the airport, that endangers or is likely to endanger safety at the airport, or

g) endangers the safety of an aircraft in flight by communicating to any other person any information that the person knows to be false,

is guilty of an indictable offence and liable to imprisonment for life. R.S., 1985, c. C-46, s. 77; 1993, c. 7, s. 3.

## Analysis of the statutes

**Match each word or phrase from the statutes on the left with a word or phrase on the right that means the same thing.**

| Word or phrase | Definition |
|---|---|
| 1. any person or property therein | a. concerning |
| 2. in respect of | b. causes a dangerous situation |
| 3. deviate in a material respect | c. serious crime (in Canada) |
| 4. thereof | d. anyone or anything in it |
| 5. in accordance with | e. cause to become |
| 6. renders | f. of it |
| 7. indictable offence | g. change a significant amount |
| 8. endangers | h. consistent with |

**Complete the following tasks:**

1. Find a section of the statutes that is focused on protecting people who respond to dangerous or violent acts on airplanes.
2. Find a section that explains which flights and aircraft these statutes apply to.
3. Find the sections or subsections that can only be violated by people who are aboard aircraft that are in flight.
4. Find the sections or subsections that can only be violated by people who are on the ground.

**Read the following hypothetical situations and answer the questions that follow. Support your answer with language from the statutes.**

Situation 1—After drinking a great deal, Oscar boarded a flight to Paris in Toronto, Canada. The flight was operated by AirFair, a budget airline headquartered in Toronto. During the meal service, the man in front of him reclined his seat all the way back. Enraged by this, Oscar began verbally abusing him. When a flight attendant attempted to intervene, Oscar wrestled him to the ground and wrapped the cord of his complementary headphones around his neck. "Fly this plane to Tucson, Arizona, where my mom lives!" he cried, "Or I'll choke him!" Alerted to the situation in the cabin, the captain decided that she had to land the plane. They were already over the open ocean. However, because they were closer to Canada than to Europe, the captain decided to turn the plane around.

About five minutes after the plane changed course, two crew members eventually succeeded in freeing the trapped attendant. In doing so, however, they dislocated Oscar's shoulder.

<u>Situation 2</u>—After drinking a great deal, Peggy boarded a GoJapan! flight from Tokyo to Vancouver. GoJapan! is a joint venture of AirFair and a Japanese airline. She continued drinking on the flight for several hours, but the crew eventually refused to serve her any more alcohol. Peggy was enraged by this. She roughly pushed the crew member who had refused to serve her out of her way, ran to one of the main exits, and tried to open it. "I'll kill us all!" she shouted, "If I just pull this lever, we'll all be sucked outside!" A number of people near the exit heard what Peggy had said, and they started to scream in panic. In fact, there was no chance that she would actually be able to open the door in flight, though she did crack some of the plastic that made up the inner portion of the door.

The crew were finally able to restrain Peggy, but she continued shouting her threats to open one of the doors. Unfortunately, it soon became apparent that she was suffering from a severe medical problem. Before the plane could make an emergency landing, Peggy had a heart attack and lost consciousness. She was revived after the plane landed.

Questions:

1. Which crimes, if any, could Oscar be charged with?
2. Which crimes, if any, could Peggy be charged with?
3. If Oscar sues the airline or the crew members for his injuries, how might they defend themselves based on these statutes?
4. If evidence shows that Peggy's confrontation with the crew brought on her heart attack, could they defend themselves based on these statutes?

## Exercise 8    Spiking drinks (Australia)

### Lead-in

**Read the extract from a newspaper article below and answer the questions:**

A 20-year-old woman from Croydon has spoken about the terrifying experience of having her drink spiked. The young woman, who hasn't been named, was at The White Horse in the center of town on Saturday night when she was attacked. She told police, "I went to the bar to get another drink, but I don't remember anything after that. I woke up in a strange place with a terrible headache, and my clothes were all over the floor." She managed to get out of the building and called the police. She was taken to hospital, where doctors confirmed her drink had been spiked with a date rape drug.

The police have been studying CCTV footage from the club and have a suspect whom they would like to question. A spokesperson for The White Horse said, "We would urge people to be cautious and keep an eye on their drinks when they are out."

1.   What is meant by having your drink "spiked"?
2.   In New South Wales, Australia, the issue of victim consent is relevant to proving a charge of rape. Why are rape cases where the victim has had their drink spiked often very complicated?
3.   Do you think drink spiking is different from simply encouraging another person to drink too much alcohol?

## Exercises

Read this extract from the New South Wales, Australia, Crimes Act 1900 No 40[10] relating to spiking drinks and answer the questions that follow.

*Crimes Act 1900 No 40*
38A Spiking drink or food
(1)  In this section—
   **harm** includes an impairment of the senses or understanding of a person that the person might reasonably be expected to object to in the circumstances.
   **impair** includes further impair.
(2)  A person—
   (a)  who causes another person to be given or to consume drink or food—
      (i)   containing an intoxicating substance that the other person is not aware it contains, or
      (ii)  containing more of an intoxicating substance than the other person would reasonably expect it to contain, and
   (b)  who intends a person to be harmed by the consumption of the drink or food,
   is guilty of an offence.

(3) For the purposes of this section, giving a person drink or food includes preparing the drink or food for the person or making it available for consumption by the person.

(4) A person does not commit an offence against this section if the person has reasonable cause to believe that each person who was likely to consume the drink or food would not have objected to consuming the drink or food if the person had been aware of the presence and quantity of the intoxicating substance in the drink or food.

(5) A person who uses an intoxicating substance in the course of any medical, dental or other health professional practice does not commit an offence against this section.

. . .

## Analysis of the statute

**Choose the best answer:**

1.  Impairment of the senses is when:
    a.  you feel stressed but do not know why.
    b.  your reaction times improve.
    c.  the power of one or more of your sensory functions (seeing, hearing, etc.) is reduced.
    d.  you temporarily lose your sense of hearing.
2.  An intoxicating substance:
    a.  enhances your ability to act and/or think.
    b.  reduces the risk of you making bad decisions.
    c.  potentially causes you to lose control of your physical and mental abilities.
    d.  boosts your immune system.

**Mark the following statements as True (T) or False (F):**

1.  If someone is already drunk when given a spiked drink, the statute would not apply. **T / F**
2.  Giving someone a large glass of whisky which they didn't know also contained a sleeping pill would be caught by section 38A(2)(a)(ii). **T / F**
3.  You don't need to intend the victim to be harmed by the spiked drink or food to be found guilty. **T / F**
4.  It is a defense to argue that you reasonably believed that the person to whom you had given a spiked drink would have accepted it even if they had known it was spiked. **T / F**

5. A dentist who drugs a patient to stop them talking while she works is unlikely to be found guilty under this statute. **T / F**

**Answer the following questions:**

1. Give an example of an impairment of the senses or understanding that a person might reasonably be expected to object to.
2. Barry and Jane are drinking in a bar together on a first date. Both have been drinking beer and feel a little drunk. Barry suggests they have a shot of flavored vodka. Jane agrees and Barry goes to the bar to buy the shots. However, before giving Jane her shot, Barry secretly puts a drug into the glass. The drug is a powerful intoxicant that is well known for being used as a "date rape" drug. Jane drinks the shot quickly and wakes up 12 hours later not remembering anything. Is Barry guilty of an offense under section 38A of the Crimes Act 1900?
3. Sarah organized the annual soccer club dinner. Fourteen of her teammates attended the event, held in the team's clubhouse. The invite specifically warned guests not to drive to the party because the objective was "to get wasted." The ladies in the team spent all evening drinking wine, beer, and spirits and were noisily drunk. Around midnight, Sarah brought out a tray of brownies and everyone ate them all very quickly. About 45 minutes later, many of the ladies started giggling uncontrollably, while others sat motionless in their chairs staring at disco lights projecting shapes on the ceiling. Sarah informed them all very loudly that she had added marijuana to the brownies. Could she be guilty of an offense under 38A of the Crimes Act 1900?

## Exercise 9    Defamation (United Kingdom)

### Lead-in

1. Why do people care about their reputations?
2. If somebody said something untrue about you to somebody else, do you think you should be able to sue them? What factors might the court consider when deciding if you are able to make a claim?
3. Do you think operators of websites should be held liable for defamatory statements published on their websites?

**Read the following text and answer the questions:**

Defamation law is a legal framework that governs statements that harm the reputation of individuals or entities (for example, companies). Defamation occurs when false statements are communicated to a third party, damaging the subject's reputation. To establish defamation in the United Kingdom, claimants must demonstrate that the statement is false, has caused harm to their reputation, and that it was communicated to a third party. Truth is a strong defense in defamation cases, and statements made in the public interest may also be protected. The burden of proof typically lies with the person who made the allegedly defamatory statement to show it was not false. Additionally, the United Kingdom recognizes qualified privileges, providing protection for certain statements made in specific contexts, such as in legal proceedings or by journalists reporting responsibly.

**Mark the following statements as True (T) or False (F):**

1. A statement can only be defamatory if it is communicated to a third person. **T / F**
2. Telling somebody else something true that damages the reputation of the subject will result in a legal liability for defamation. **T / F**
3. The subject of the alleged defamation must prove that the statement is false. **T / F**

**Read this extract from UK Defamation Act 2013[11] and answer the questions that follow.**

### Defamation Act 2013

*1 Serious harm*

(1) A statement is not defamatory unless its publication has caused or is likely to cause serious harm to the reputation of the claimant.
(2) For the purposes of this section, harm to the reputation of a body that trades for profit is not "serious harm" unless it has caused or is likely to cause the body serious financial loss.

*2 Truth*

(1) It is a defence to an action for defamation for the defendant to show that the imputation conveyed by the statement complained of is substantially true.
(2) Subsection (3) applies in an action for defamation if the statement complained of conveys two or more distinct imputations.
(3) If one or more of the imputations is not shown to be substantially true, the defence under this section does not fail if, having regard to the imputations which are shown to be substantially true, the imputations which are not shown to be substantially true do not seriously harm the claimant's reputation.

. . .

*5  Operators of websites*

(1)  This section applies where an action for defamation is brought against the operator of a website in respect of a statement posted on the website.

(2)  It is a defence for the operator to show that it was not the operator who posted the statement on the website.

(3)  The defence is defeated if the claimant shows that—

    (a)  it was not possible for the claimant to identify the person who posted the statement,

    (b)  the claimant gave the operator a notice of complaint in relation to the statement, and

    (c)  the operator failed to respond to the notice of complaint in accordance with any provision contained in regulations.

. . .

## Analysis of the statute

1.  Find the word or phrase in the text that has the same or substantially the same meaning as:
    - a business entity, such as a company
    - the meaning conveyed by the publication of words or writing
2.  Why might a company not be able to win compensation under the statute for a defamatory statement made about it?
3.  What do you need to show to benefit from the defense of truth under the statute? What parts of the defense may be open to interpretation?
4.  What defense does an operator of a website have concerning defamatory statements posted on the web?
5.  What would a claimant need to show to defeat the defense of a website operator?

**Write a short paragraph answering the question based on the following facts:**

You are a volunteer for the environmental charity Greenpeace. Recently, you have been involved in a campaign highlighting environmental damage done by a UK company that is disposing of its chemical waste in a local river. During the campaign, you find out that the chairman of the company has been using the company helicopter to go on golf holidays, and you think this may be a chance to embarrass the chairman and the company and get them some negative publicity. You write a social media post, using your own name, claiming that the helicopter has flown the chairman on golf holidays 10 times in the last 12 months. You conclude by stating that the company and the chairman are enemies of the planet and should be boycotted. Both the chairman and the company sue you and the website where you made the post for defamation. It turns out the helicopter was used just six times, always with the knowledge of the company's board of directors. Although the lawsuit generates lots of publicity, the company's sales are not affected.

What is your legal position? Does the website have any potential liability?

## Exercise 10    Animal cruelty (Australia)

Read this extract from Northern Territory, Australia, Animal Protection Act 2018[12] and answer the questions that follow.

### Lead-in

There are certain medical procedures that pet owners commonly have done to their pets in order to make them easier to live with or just to improve their appearance. Some of them are mentioned in the statutes given below.

Before you read them, complete the following sentences by filling in the blanks with the appropriate word, or words, in the box.

| | | | |
|---|---|---|---|
| tail docked | horse firing | ears cropped | declawed |

1. To have an animal's ______ ______ means to remove a portion of it.
2. If an owner is worried about their cat scratching their furniture, they may have it ______.
3. ______ ______ is a technique that involves applying high heat to a leg to stimulate healing.
4. A dog owner may have their pet's ______ ______ in order to improve its appearance.

## Australia Northern Territory

### ANIMAL PROTECTION ACT 2018 (NO 25 OF 2018)—SECT 24

*Cruelty to an animal*
(1)  A person commits an offence if:
    (a)  the person intentionally engages in conduct; and
    (b)  the conduct results in the suffering of an animal, or additional suffering of an animal, and the person is reckless in relation to that result; and

   (c) the suffering is unjustifiable, unnecessary or unreasonable and the person is reckless in relation to that circumstance.

. . .

(6) A person commits an offence if:
   (a) the person is in control of an animal; and
   (b) the animal is suffering and the person knows that it is suffering; and
   (c) the person intentionally fails to take action that:
      (i) is reasonable in the circumstances; and
      (ii) the person knows would alleviate the animal's suffering.

*Examples for subsection (6)(c)*

1   *The person does not obtain necessary veterinary treatment for the animal.*
2   *The person does not destroy a suffering animal so it dies quickly without further suffering.*

(7) A person commits an offence if the person intentionally:
   (a) docks the tail of an animal; or
   (b) crops the ears of an animal; or
   (c) removes the claws of an animal; or
   (d) removes the voice of an animal; or
   (e) engages in horse firing.

(8) Subsection (7) does not apply if the person is a veterinarian who believes on reasonable grounds that the procedure is a reasonable and necessary therapeutic measure for the treatment or welfare of the animal.

## Analysis of the statute

**Choose the best answer:**

1. Suppose a veterinarian engages in horse firing and is reported to the authorities by someone who believes that this is a cruel treatment. Has she definitely violated subsection (7)?
   a.  Yes she has, because (7)(e) bans this cruel practice.
   b.  Yes she has, because she violated subsections (7)(e) and (6).
   c.  Not if she can show that she was not in control of the animal.
   d.  Not if she can show that she met the requirements of subsection (8)

2. A man is upset that his neighbor's dog constantly digs up his garden. So, he leaves out food that contains chocolate for the dog. The man knows that chocolate is toxic to dogs. After the dog returns home, he suffers from severe vomiting and diarrhea. Which subsection of the statute has the man violated?

    a.  (1)
    b.  (6)
    c.  (7)
    d.  (1)(b)

3. Assume the same facts as in question 2. After the dog returns home, his owner sees the dog in distress but puts off taking him to the vet for several hours because she thinks that she will have difficulty paying the bill. Which subsection, if any, has she potentially violated?
   a. (1)
   b. (6)
   c. She has not violated any subsection because her behavior was reasonable.
   d. She cannot be prosecuted because her neighbor is responsible for poisoning the dog.

**Mark the following statements as True (T) or False (F):**

1. Under section 24(1) of the Act, a person can be found to have committed the offense if it is proved their conduct came within 24(1)(a) and (b). **T / F**
2. Under section 24(1) of the Act, a person can be found guilty even if they did not intend to cause an animal's suffering. **T / F**
3. A person can be found guilty under section 24(6) of the Act only if they know an animal is suffering. **T / F**
4. Section 24(6) of the Act only applies when a person fails to take an animal that is suffering to a vet. **T / F**
5. A vet could be protected under section 24(8) if they cropped a dog's ear that was badly infected. **T / F**

**Choose the response that best answers the questions below.**

1. Tommy drives to a restaurant for lunch with friends. His dog comes with him. When he arrives, he finds that the restaurant will not accept dogs, so he leaves him in the car. He completely forgets to leave a window open, even though it is 104 °F. When he returns three hours later, his dog has died of heat stroke. Is Tommy liable under section 24 of the Animal Protection Act 2018?
   a. Tommy did not have the requisite intention under the Act to be found guilty because he loved his dog very much and had no idea he could die just from being locked in a hot car.
   b. Tommy never intended to leave his dog in the car and only did so because the restaurant didn't accept the dog inside. Therefore, he cannot be guilty.

   c. Tommy is most likely liable because he intended to leave the dog in the car and was reckless about the possible consequences. The death was unjustifiable, unnecessary, and unreasonable.

   d. Although he was reckless leaving his dog in a hot car, it cannot be said the death was unjustifiable, unnecessary, or unreasonable because Tommy had no other choice because of the restaurant's rules.

2. Sophie was duck hunting with a friend when the friend accidentally shot a cow eating grass on the other side of the riverbank. She saw through her binoculars that the cow had been shot in the back and was lying down, clearly in distress. Worried the police would find out she had forgotten to renew her gun license, she immediately left the area with her friend in a panic and did not notify anybody of the accident. Could she be liable under section 24 of the Animal Protection Act 2018?

   a. Since she was not responsible for shooting the cow, the Act could not ever apply to Sophie.

   b. Although she knew the cow was suffering and took no steps to help it, she would probably not be liable under section 24(6) because she was not "in control" of the cow.

   c. Since she had recklessly allowed her gun license to expire, she could be held liable under section 24(1).

   d. She did not call a vet even though she knew it would help the cow, so she would most likely be convicted under section 24(6).

3. Mehtap's cat likes to scratch its claws on the furniture while she is out at work. The cat has caused thousands of dollars' worth of damage, so Mehtap asks her friend, who is a vet, to remove the cat's claws. This solves the problem, but an anonymous call has been made to the animal protection authorities making a complaint about this. Who could be found liable under section 24 of the Animal Protection Act 2018?

   a. Although her friend was a vet, it is unlikely he could show it was reasonable and necessary for the treatment or welfare of Mehtap's cat. Therefore, he is likely to be held liable under section 24(7).

   b. Mehtap would most likely be convicted under section 24 of the Act because she allowed her friend to remove the cat's claws.

   c. Although both Mehtap and her friend would appear to be subject to section 24(7), they could benefit from the provisions in section 24(8) because the friend is a vet.

   d. Both Mehtap and her friend would most likely be found guilty of an offense under section 24(1).

**Answer the questions using full sentences. Make references to the Animal Protection Act 2018 where appropriate.**

1.  How might you commit an offense under the Act even if you had no intention of causing harm or suffering to an animal? You may use one or more examples to illustrate your point.
2.  Some dogs have traditionally had their tails cut ("docked") for cosmetic purposes. Does the Act apply in such cases?

## Exercise 11    Burglary (United States)[13]

### Lead-in

Read the common law definition of burglary below and then answer the following questions:

1.  Does the common law require a person to actually commit a crime inside someone's home in order to be guilty of burglary?
2.  What do you think "breaking" means? Why do you think the common law requires it?
3.  What do you think the purpose is of the "at night" requirement?
4.  Can you think of any public policy reasons why legislatures might eliminate these last two requirements?

The common law definition of burglary requires (1) breaking, (2) into someone else's home, (3) at night, (4) with the intention of committing a theft or a felony inside.[14] However, most common law jurisdictions now define burglary by statute. In this exercise, you will compare and analyze several of these statutes.

The approaches that American states take to defining burglary are quite varied. Here are some examples:

<u>Washington</u> defines "residential burglary" in Revised Code of Washington section 9A.52.025:

(1)  A person is guilty of residential burglary if, with intent to commit a crime against a person or property therein, the person enters or remains unlawfully in a dwelling other than a vehicle.

<u>Maine</u> defines burglary in Criminal Code section 401 as follows:

1.  A person is guilty of burglary if:
    A.  The person enters or surreptitiously remains in a structure knowing that that person is not licensed or privileged to do so, with the intent to commit a crime therein.

In <u>Louisiana</u>, "simple burglary" is defined by section 14:62 of the Louisiana Revised Statutes:

A.  Simple burglary is the unauthorized entering of any dwelling, vehicle, watercraft, or other structure, movable or immovable, or any cemetery, with the intent to commit a felony or any theft therein . . .

Statutes now define burglary in common law jurisdictions outside of the United States as well. In the <u>United Kingdom</u>, for example, burglary is defined by the Theft Act 1968:

(1)  A person is guilty of burglary if—
    (a)  he enters any building or part of a building as a trespasser and with intent to commit any such offence as is mentioned in subsection (2) below; or
    (b)  having entered any building or part of a building as a trespasser he steals or attempts to steal anything in the building or that part of it or inflicts or attempts to inflict on any person therein any grievous bodily harm.
(2)  The offences referred to in subsection (1)(a) above are offences of stealing anything in the building or part of a building in question, of inflicting on any person therein any grievous bodily harm therein, and of doing unlawful damage to the building or anything therein.

## Analysis of the statutes

**Choose the best answer:**

1.  A "dwelling" is a place where a person ______.
    a.  works
    b.  studies
    c.  lives
    d.  hides
2.  To do something "surreptitiously" means to do it ______.
    a.  intentionally
    b.  nocturnally
    c.  unlawfully
    d.  secretly
3.  The Washington statute refers to a person who "enters or remains unlawfully in a dwelling . . . ." What word or phrase in the UK statute comes closest in meaning to this language?
    a.  he enters any building
    b.  trespasser

    c.   building in question

    d.   therein

4.  In the Maine statute above, the word "therein" refers back to the word _____.

    a.   person

    b.   structure

    c.   crime

    d.   license

## Application of the statutes to facts

**<u>Based only on the language of the statutes provided</u>, answer the questions below:**

1. Can you come up with a set of facts that would constitute burglary under all of these statutes, but not under the common law definition?
2. An archeologist enters a sealed tomb without authorization. The tomb is built above ground and is tall enough for an average person to stand upright in. They are looking for treasure that they believe was buried along with its owner. In which jurisdictions would the archeologist be guilty of burglary?
3. The same facts as in question 2, but the archeologist digs up an ordinary grave in a graveyard.
4. Can you come up with a set of facts that would constitute burglary in Washington and Maine, but not in Louisiana or the United Kingdom?
5. Which statutes might be violated by a person who breaks into a locked car?
6. A person buys a flatbed truck. They build a "tiny house" on the back of it and make this their permanent residence. A person enters the house with the intention to commit theft inside. Under which statutes would they be guilty?
7. Imagine that a person enters a computer store without the intention to steal anything. Once inside, they see an expensive computer and decide to steal it. If they steal it during the hours when the store is open, would they violate any of the statutes?
8. The same facts as in question 7, but the person hides in the store until after it closes before stealing the computer.
9. A group of young teenagers enters an abandoned house, looking for a place where they can drink without being caught by their parents. Once inside, they get into an argument. One boy hits another with an empty bottle, causing lacerations that require stitches. Is he guilty of burglary under any of the statutes?

## Exercise 12    Corporate liability for causing harm (miscellaneous jurisdictions)

Lead-in

**Read the following text and consider the questions that follow:**

The Bhopal disaster, which occurred on December 3, 1984, was one of the world's worst industrial disasters. A pesticide plant owned by Union Carbide Corporation in Bhopal, India, leaked toxic methyl isocyanate gas, resulting in the deaths of thousands and causing long-term health issues for many more. The disaster led to widespread criticism of Union Carbide for inadequate safety measures and negligence. In 1989, the company reached a settlement with the Indian government for $470 million, a sum criticized as insufficient given the scale of the tragedy. The issue of corporate responsibility and accountability for the Bhopal disaster remains controversial, with ongoing debates about justice and the need for stronger regulations in industrial safety.

1.   Do you think companies should be held legally responsible for causing the death of someone?
2.   What do you think are the difficulties in successfully prosecuting a corporation for causing harm or even the death of a person?

The following statutes from different common law jurisdictions all impose criminal liability on corporations for causing harm to people. Read them and answer the questions that follow.

### Canada Criminal Code R.S.C., 1985, c. C-46[15]

*Duty of persons directing work*
217.1 Every one* who undertakes, or has the authority, to direct how another person does work or performs a task is under a legal duty to take reasonable steps to prevent bodily harm to that person, or any other person, arising from that work or task. 2003, c. 21, s. 3.

### UK Corporate Manslaughter and Corporate Homicide Act 2007[16]

1    The offence
   (1)   An organisation to which this section applies is guilty of an offence if the way in which its activities are managed or organised—
      (a)   causes a person's death, and

---

* includes a corporation pursuant to 22.1 and 22.2 of the Criminal Code of Canada

(b) amounts to a gross breach of a relevant duty of care owed by the organisation to the deceased.

. . .

(3) An organisation is guilty of an offence under this section only if the way in which its activities are managed or organised by its senior management is a substantial element in the breach referred to in subsection (1).

. . .

## Australia Northern Territory S34B Work Health And Safety (National Uniform Legislation) Act 2011[17]

*34B Industrial Manslaughter*
(1) A person* commits the offence of industrial manslaughter if:
   (a) the person has a health and safety duty; and
   (b) the person is a person conducting a business or undertaking or an officer of a person conducting a business or undertaking; and
   (c) the person intentionally engages in conduct; and
   (d) the conduct breaches the health and safety duty and causes the death of an individual to whom the health and safety duty is owed; and
   (e) the person is reckless or negligent about the conduct breaching the health and safety duty and causing the death of that individual.

. . .

(4) For this section, a person's conduct causes death if it substantially contributes to the death.

## Analysis of the statutes

**Match the following words/phrases with the correct definition:**

| Word or phrase | Definition |
| --- | --- |
| 1. duty of care | a. actions that are sensible and appropriate in order to achieve a certain goal or comply with a requirement |
| 2. engages in conduct | b. plays a significant role in causing something |
| 3. reasonable steps | c. participates in behavior or actions |
| 4. substantially contributes to | d. key management executives who carry out the daily work of a business |
| 5. breach | e. the legal responsibility to take reasonable care to avoid causing harm or injury to others |
| 6. officer | f. a failure to fulfill a legal obligation, duty, or agreement |

---

* includes a corporation pursuant to Part IIAA of the Criminal Code of the Northern Territory

**Mark the following statements as True (T) or False (F):**

1. The Canada Criminal Code R.S.C., 1985, c. C-46 imposes duties on every person working with other people. **T / F**
2. To be guilty of an offense under the UK Corporate Manslaughter and Corporate Homicide Act 2007, you must satisfy the requirements of section 1 (1)(a) and (b). **T / F**
3. Under the Corporate Manslaughter and Corporate Homicide Act 2007, an organization can be held guilty of an offense if any employee's conduct is a substantial element in the death of another person. **T / F**
4. Under section 34B of the Australia Northern Territory S34B Work Health And Safety (National Uniform Legislation) Act 2011, a person would commit an offense if one of the elements listed in section 34B(1) (a) through (e) is proved. **T / F**
5. All the statutes only apply if a person dies. **T / F**
6. All the statutes involve some sort of breach of a legal duty by a person or corporation managing the work of an individual. **T / F**
7. Each statute requires that any breach be a significant factor in any harm caused to an individual. **T / F**

**Imagine that the following scenarios take place in each of the jurisdictions in which the statutes are in force (United Kingdom, Canada, and the Northern Territory of Australia). What would be the outcome in respect of each one? Answer using details from the respective statutes, giving reasons for your answer.**

1. ABC Construction Limited has a detailed written health and safety policy, including the requirement for all workers to wear harnesses at all times on construction sites. However, the managing director—who is also the majority shareholder of the company—is worried that the firm is close to going out of business and tells all site foremen that in order to save costs, old harnesses should not be replaced. One of the workers, Bob, falls from the second floor of a building when his old harness breaks during a routine operation that he is carrying out in accordance with building safety standards. He suffers a permanent disability and must use a wheelchair for the rest of his life.
2. Pat works as a long-distance truck driver for a courier company. The regulations state that she must have 45 minutes of rest after 4.5 hours of driving and that no journey can take more than 10 hours in total. Her company handbook instructs her to follow these regulations. However, her company also pays her a 5% bonus if she arrives early to make deliveries. Therefore,

she often misses her breaks. Her boss knows this from the electronic tracking of her truck and has asked her to be more careful. On one trip of more than 1000 km, Pat takes just one 15-minute stop, during which she drinks one liter of beer. One hour later, she falls asleep at the wheel of the truck and is killed in an accident. Could Pat's employer be held liable?

## Exercise 13    Marriage to a first cousin (United States)

Most American states place restrictions on marriage between close relatives, though where they draw the line can vary significantly. Read the following statutes about marriage between first cousins and then complete the exercises that follow.

### Lead-in

1.  What public good could justify banning marriage between close cousins?
2.  What exceptions do the statutes make? Do these make sense, given the purpose of the statutes?
3.  Some of the statutes deal with activity that takes place in other states. What is their concern?

### Arizona

A.R.S. § 25-101 (2010)
Void and prohibited marriages

A.  Marriage between parents and children, including grandparents and grandchildren of every degree . . . and between uncles and nieces, aunts and nephews and between first cousins, is prohibited and void.
B.  Notwithstanding subsection A, first cousins may marry if both are sixty-five years of age or older or if one or both first cousins are under sixty-five years of age, upon approval of any superior court judge in the state if proof has been presented to the judge that one of the cousins is unable to reproduce.

. . .

A.R.S. § 25-112 (2010)
Marriages contracted in another state; validity and effect

A.  Marriages valid by the laws of the place where contracted are valid in this state, except marriages that are void and prohibited by section 25–101.

B.  Marriages solemnized in another state or country by parties intending at the time to reside in this state shall have the same legal consequences and effect as if solemnized in this state, except marriages that are void and prohibited by section 25–101.

C.  Parties residing in this state may not evade the laws of this state relating to marriage by going to another state or country for solemnization of the marriage.

## Indiana

IN Code § 31-11-1-2 (2010)
Two (2) individuals may not marry each other if the individuals are more closely related than second cousins. However, two (2) individuals may marry each other if the individuals are:

(1)  first cousins; and
(2)  both at least sixty-five (65) years of age.

## Maine

MRS Title 19-A, §701.
Prohibited marriages; exceptions

1.  Marriage out of State to evade law. When residents of this State, with intent to evade this section and to return and reside here, go into another state or country to have their marriage solemnized there and afterwards return and reside here, that marriage is void in this State.

1-A. Certain marriages performed in another state not recognized in this State. Any marriage performed in another state that would violate any provisions of subsections 2 to 4 if performed in this State is not recognized in this State and is considered void if the parties take up residence in this State.

2.  Prohibitions based on degrees of consanguinity; exceptions. This subsection governs marriage between relatives.

    A.  A man may not marry his mother, grandmother, daughter, granddaughter, sister, brother's daughter, sister's daughter, father's sister, mother's sister, the daughter of his father's brother or sister or the daughter of his mother's brother or sister. A woman may not marry her father, grandfather, son, grandson, brother, brother's son, sister's son, father's brother, mother's brother, the son of her father's brother or sister or the son of her mother's brother or sister. A person may not marry that person's parent, grandparent, child, grandchild, sibling, nephew, niece, aunt or uncle.

B.  Notwithstanding paragraph A, a man may marry the daughter of his father's brother or sister or the daughter of his mother's brother or sister, and a woman may marry the son of her father's brother or sister or the son of her mother's brother or sister as long as . . . the man or woman provides [a] physician's certificate of genetic counseling.

## New Jersey

NJ Rev Stat § 37:1-1 (2022)
Certain marriages or civil unions prohibited.

d.  No person shall marry or enter into a civil union with any of the person's ancestors or descendants, or the person's sibling, or the child of the person's sibling, or the sibling of the person's parent, whether such collateral kindred be of the whole or half blood.

e.  A marriage or civil union in violation of subsection d. of this section shall be absolutely void.

## North Carolina

N.C. Gen. Stat. § 51-3 (2010)
All marriages between any two persons nearer of kin than first cousins, or between double first cousins . . . shall be void. No marriage followed by cohabitation and the birth of issue shall be declared void after the death of either of the parties for any of the causes stated in this section except for bigamy. . . .

## Wisconsin

Wis. Stat. § 765.03
No marriage shall be contracted while either of the parties has a spouse living, nor between persons who are nearer of kin than second cousins, except that marriage may be contracted between first cousins where the female has attained the age of 55 or where either party submits an affidavit signed by a physician stating that either party is permanently sterile.

## Analysis of the statute

**Match the word on the left with the definition on the right.**

| Word or phrase | Definition |
| --- | --- |
| 1.  kin | a.  to perform a ceremony |
| 2.  void | b.  a child of your aunt or uncle |
| 3.  sibling | c.  not able to create children |
| 4.  incest | d.  a person's brother or sister |
| 5.  cousin | e.  unable to have sex |
| 6.  sterile | f.  having a common ancestor |
| 7.  impotent | g.  sex between closely related people |
| 8.  solemnize | h.  to escape or avoid something |
| 9.  to evade | i.  an indirect blood relationship |
| 10. consanguinity | j.  a person's relatives |
| 11. collateral kinship | k.  having no legal effect |

**Choose the best answer:**

1.  NJ Rev Stat § 37:1-1 (2022) states that "No person shall marry or enter into a civil union with any of the person's *ancestors.*" That means, among other things, that the person cannot marry his or her ______.
    a.  cousin
    b.  child
    c.  parent
    d.  spouse
2.  What does the phrase "half blood" mean in the same statute?
    a.  related by marriage
    b.  sharing no parents
    c.  not related by blood
    d.  sharing one parent
3.  Both Arizona's A.R.S. § 25-101 (2010) and Maine's MRS Title 19-A, §701, use the word "notwithstanding." What is the purpose of the word in both statutes?
    a.  It introduces an exception to a general rule.
    b.  It is used to give an illustration of a rule.
    c.  It is a synonym for the phrase "in addition."
    d.  It introduces the main purpose of the statute.

4. Choose the best paraphrase of the phrase "cohabitation and the birth of issue" in N.C. Gen. Stat. § 51-3 (2010):
   a. living together and planning a family
   b. living together and having a baby
   c. forming a habit and creating an issue
   d. marriage and the beginning of pregnancy

**Based only on the language of the statutes provided, answer the questions below.**

1. In which states, if any, may first cousins generally marry each other?
2. Are there any states where first cousins may never marry under any circumstances?
3. Could two first cousins from Arizona get married in New Jersey and then have the marriage recognized by their home state?
4. Imagine that two brothers from one family marry two sisters from another family. Is there any jurisdiction where the marriage of a child of one couple to the child of the other couple could be valid?
5. Same situation as in question 3. Is there any situation in which this marriage would not be void in North Carolina?
6. A 60-year-old woman wants to marry her first cousin—a 57-year-old man. In which states could this be legal?
7. If two first cousins are married in a state that allows such a marriage, under what circumstances could they have their marriage recognized in Maine?
8. Come up with a scenario where two first cousins, who are married in a state that allows such a marriage, could have their marriage recognized in Maine, but not in Arizona.

## Conclusion

If you have worked your way through all or many of the exercises in this chapter, you will have practiced a lot of the key skills you need to interpret common law statutes effectively. In particular, you will have practiced doing the following:

- Analyzing the organization of statutes, including sections, subsections, and headings.
- Identifying the purpose and structure of different parts within a statute.
- Identifying and interpreting cross-references within statutes.
- Extracting the main legal principles and obligations from a given statute.
- Recognizing and comprehending specialized legal terminology commonly used in common law statutes.

- Differentiating between mandatory and permissive language within statutory provisions.
- Articulating the purpose and effect of specific statutory provisions.
- Applying the provisions of a statute to the facts of a hypothetical situation to solve a legal problem.

It bears repeating that there is really no substitute for close reading when it comes to working out the meaning of a statute so that it can be applied when solving legal problems. The good news is that you will become much more proficient at doing it with a lot of practice.

## Chapter 2
## Reading Cases

As you saw in chapter 1, there is more to law in common law systems than just cases. Still, court decisions are clearly more important in common law than in civil law. There is also no denying that case law is generally the thing that students from civil law countries are most apprehensive about when they start studying common law. Hopefully, by the end of this chapter, most of that apprehension will have gone away. The chapter contains a number of simple cases, from appellate courts in a variety of jurisdictions, as well as exercises to help you read and analyze them. You will notice that many of these cases are matters of criminal law rather than civil law (in the other sense of the phrase "civil law"). There is no particular reason for this other than criminal cases often tend to have slightly more engaging facts for students. However, the skills you practice working on these criminal cases apply just as equally to civil law cases. You will also be introduced to a note-taking technique that will help you identify the basic elements of a case, understand them, and remember them: the "case brief." Although case briefing is an important tool, ultimately you will find that, as with statutes, successfully analyzing cases is mostly a matter of careful, thoughtful reading.

## Common law

The cases in this chapter, as well as cases in general, can be divided into two types: cases interpreting statutes, and cases based purely on other cases.[1]

The latter kind of cases are known as "common law." At this point, it is probably a good idea to clarify a confusing piece of terminology: The term "common law" can mean a system of law (or a family of legal systems); it can also mean the particular kind of law that makes this system unique.[2] Civil law lawyers will often have learned that common law, in the latter sense, has something to do with "customary law," as that term is understood in civil law jurisdictions. We would suggest that it is probably best to avoid falling back on civil law categories while working with common law. To avoid confusion, it is best to start from scratch and to think of it as a new kind of law without any real civil law equivalent.

You have probably heard that "common law" involves reasoning from case to case in a way that is quite different than the way courts reason and write in your jurisdiction.[3] In reality, this kind of reasoning is quite intuitive, and indeed, familiar. This is because it is a very common way for humans to make and communicate rules in a wide variety of situations.

For example, imagine that a student goes to their instructor's office and asks for extra time to complete an assignment.[4] Imagine that the instructor rejects this request and justifies his decision by saying that the student has had plenty of time to prepare the assignment. Imagine further that the student tells the other students in the class of the instructor's decision, and the reasoning behind it. It would, then, be clear to everyone that the rule in the class is that "no extra time will be given for assignments." In fact, if another student then went to the instructor and asked for the same thing, we would probably think that their behavior was rather strange; clearly, the instructor's decision about the one student was meant to express the rule that applied to everyone in the class in substantially the same situation.

Nevertheless, we would not find it odd at all if another student went to the instructor with an excuse, in an attempt to distinguish their case from that of the student before them. For example, if this student had been ill for a significant part of the time given to do the assignment, she might argue that her situation was quite different from that of the first student, and that the instructor's prior decision and reasoning should not apply to her.

If the instructor accepted that excuse, and if the other students found out about it, they would understand that the rule for their course had been expanded and clarified a bit. Naturally, they would understand the new rule to be something like "No extra time will be given for assignments without a legitimate excuse." Furthermore, they would all realize that if they wanted extra time as well, they would do well to explain how their own situation was importantly analogous to that of the second student.

As you may know, the reasoning in the previous paragraphs is a form of inductive reasoning. It begins with a decision made in a particular case (here, the decision to deny the first student extra time), from which a rule must be extracted (students have had enough time to do the assignment and will not be given any more) and applied to similar situations.

The point of the example in the preceding paragraphs is that everyone uses this sort of reasoning every day. We are also well acquainted with the kind of argument used by the second student, who convinced the instructor that her case was different than a case where the rule was not in her favor, and we can easily imagine how other students might rely on the decision made in her case. As you will see as you work your way through the chapter, this kind of argument, by distinction and analogy, is all that is really meant by "reasoning from case to case."

## Cases interpreting statutes

You probably assume that the cases in this chapter interpreting statutory law will look a lot like the cases that you have studied in your home jurisdiction. To some extent, this is probably true. In this chapter, you will see judges trying to determine the meaning of statutory provisions by looking at the plain meaning of words in the text, examining the purpose that the provisions are supposed to promote, and other kinds of analysis that will probably seem familiar to you. However, even in cases based on statutes, there are important differences between civil and common law practice.

First of all, you may have noted in chapter 1 that common law statutes themselves can look quite different than the codes of your own jurisdiction. Quite often, they will be rather vaguer and more open-ended. This is due to a difference in ideology: while in civil law a code is meant to be a complete, comprehensive statement of the law, common law statutes are written by legislators who accept the role of the courts in developing the law. These legislators write statutes under the assumption that the courts will almost certainly add the granular detail of the law later, in decisions on individual cases. In other words, the codes are incomplete statements of the law basically by design.

Secondly, you will probably notice that courts do not always take the opinions of legal scholars into account when making their decisions. Whether a court is interpreting a statute or a purely common law matter, prior precedents, not scholarly articles, are the first source that a court looks to in making its decision. Indeed, they must do so when the precedents are binding. (It is a feature of the common law that decisions made in higher courts bind judges in lower courts, i.e., lower courts *must* follow the law set out in those decisions when deciding cases of a similar nature. This doctrine, known by the Latin term *stare decisis*, is at the heart of the common law and the principal reason cases are so important.) Thus, even when a case is based on statute law, most of the opinion will generally consist of citations to cases, and the court will engage in the same kind of reasoning from one case to another that characterizes opinions based solely on common law.[5]

## Case briefing

Despite all of these important differences, there is no reason that you shouldn't be able to learn to interpret cases fairly quickly. In order to help you to learn how to do so, this chapter will introduce you to a method of note-taking known as a "case brief." The point of the brief is to identify and analyze the main sections of a case. Although there is no one way of briefing a case, the case briefing structure that you will learn in this chapter contains basic elements that will, in some form, be part of the case briefs that students typically learn in the legal writing programs of LL.M. degrees:

1.  Procedural history—This is the story that the court tells about the path of the dispute as it moves through the court system. It includes details like the cause of action, criminal charges, which party has appealed the judgment, and what they are asking for.
2.  Facts—This is the story of the dispute itself; the things that happened out in the world that resulted in a civil lawsuit or public prosecution.
3.  Issue—This is the question that the court has to answer in order to solve the case. (Most modern cases will involve a number of issues. However, we have either chosen simple one-issue cases or edited more complex cases for brevity in order to help you master the basic techniques without becoming overwhelmed by complexities.)
4.  Holding—This is the resolution of the issue. Combined with the reasoning, it is the part of the case that can be applied in future cases as binding law.
5.  Reasoning—In order for a case to serve as a useful precedent, the court must explain why it resolved the issue the way that it did.

At first, you may struggle to correctly identify all of these parts. There are, however, a few language clues that you can look out for while reading. For example, when discussing both the procedural history and the facts, a court will generally use the simple past tense. Another grammatical clue to look for is that when a court is explaining its own thinking—such as when it is stating a holding—it will often use the first-person plural (e.g., "We hold that" or "We find that"). In addition, when introducing the issue, a court will often begin by stating the legal position of the party who has brought the case before it, so look for sentences starting with "Appellant contends," "Appellant argues," or similar phrases. When a court is explaining its reasoning, it will generally discuss the existing law, so reasoning sections will contain many citations to statutes and precedent.

All of the pieces of a case are important, and none can be ignored. Still, it is probably safe to say that the key to analyzing a case is figuring out the issue(s). If you can do this, most of the rest of the case should fall into place pretty easily. In analyzing the issue, it is important to look beyond the surface. For example, in a burglary case, a student might initially think: "The issue is whether the defendant is guilty of burglary." To answer this question, however, the court will have to decide a deeper question, such as what particular words in a statute mean. In one California case, for instance, the appellant had been convicted of burglary after inserting someone else's bank card into an ATM machine built into the wall of a bank. He contended that his conviction had to be reversed because the ATM was not a "building" under the burglary statute, and that, in any event, he had not "entered" it because the card left his hand and was out of his control while it was in the machine.[6] These questions, the meaning of "building" and "entry" under the statute, are the real issues. If you can spot these and articulate them, then you are well on your way to understanding the whole case.

In summary, although the cases in this chapter may be somewhat different than those that you might have read in the past, none of the knowledge needed to interpret them is especially complex or difficult to understand. All that you need are a few strategies to make it a bit easier, and the willingness to read carefully.

By the end of the chapter, you should hopefully be able to do the following:

- Identify the key legal concepts and principles of a point of law from reading a case (also known as an "opinion").
- Identify the structure of a case, including the procedural history, case facts, legal issues, decision, and reasoning.
- Recognize and comprehend specialized legal terminology commonly used in common law case law.
- Construct a case brief with its necessary structural components (procedural history, case facts, legal issues, decision, and reasoning).

## Exercise 1    Appeal cases

### Lead-in

In the introduction to this chapter, you read about the importance of cases. As part of this, the concept of *stare decisis* was briefly mentioned. This is the distinctive part of the common law, where lower courts *must* follow the law set out in decisions made by higher courts when making judgments about cases that have similar facts.

All the cases in the exercises that follow record decisions made by higher courts. In effect, these cases are making law by interpreting statutes, the decisions of other courts, or both. Before we start looking at the cases in detail, let's do some brief work on some important vocabulary that you will come across a lot in the exercises that follow. You will notice that some words have specific meanings in US and UK courts, which can be a bit confusing. Be careful to note which jurisdiction applies when you are doing the exercises!

**Match the following words with the correct definition:**

| Word | Definition |
| --- | --- |
| 1. appeal | a. to accept an appeal against a lower court decision |
| 2. appellant | b. to reject an appeal |
| 3. hold | c. to confirm or uphold the original decision of the court that is being appealed |
| 4. affirm (US) | d. (to make) a formal request to the court for a decision to be changed or reversed |
| 5. dismiss (UK) | e. to make a decision in a legal case |
| 6. allow (UK) | f. the person/party who makes an appeal to the court |
| 7. reverse (US) | g. to change the decision of the original court |

**Use the words from the box to complete the sentences below. You may need to change the form of the word.**

1.  The New York appellate judge ______ the lower court's ruling, stating that it had correctly interpreted the key precedent when coming to its decision.
2.  The UK Court of Appeal ruled against the ______ and upheld the decision of the trial court.
3.  The appeal by the defendant was ______ on the basis that the trial judge had correctly directed the jury as to the meaning of "reckless" in the statute.
4.  The court ______ that no entry to a dwelling had been made.

5. The UK Supreme Court _______ the appeal on the grounds that the trial judge had made an error of law with regard to consent.
6. The trial court's decision was _______ by the California Court of Appeal and the defendant's conviction quashed.
7. The defendant _______ to the higher court to overturn his conviction.

## Exercise 2   Example of a case interpreting a statute (United States)

### Lead-in

Although this chapter is primarily about reading and understanding cases, we are going to start with some exercises that aim to show how some cases relate to the interpretation of a statute. Therefore, to begin, complete the statute below with words from the box.

**Fill in the blanks with one of the words below:**

| | | | |
|---|---|---|---|
| vandalism | penal | defaces | real |
| graffiti | maliciously | acts | |

California _______ Code § 594

(a) Every person who _______ commits any of the following _______ with respect to any _______ or personal property not his or her own . . . is guilty of _______ :

(1) _______ with _______ or other inscribed material, [or]
(2) Damages [or]
(3) Destroys.

**In the exercise below, a paragraph from the *In re Nicholas Y.* case has been broken into sentences, and each sentence has been paraphrased in simpler language. Match each original sentence with the paraphrase that expresses the same idea. (You may wish to refer back to this exercise when reading the case.)**

1. _______Appellant contends he did not violate the statute because the word "deface" [means] a "permanent alteration" of the surface of an object rather than the easily removed marking he placed on the window.
2. _______He compares the facts of this case to chalk writing on a sidewalk held not to constitute vandalism in violation of Penal Code section 594 in *Mackinney v. Nielsen* 69 F.3d 1002 (9th Cir.1995).

3.   _____As appellant acknowledges, however, the statutory language inter-
     preted in that case was different, making it "illegal to (1) *deface 'with paint
     or any other liquid,'* (2) damage or (3) destroy any real or personal prop-
     erty that is not one's own." (*Id.* at p. 1005, emphasis added.)
4.   _____The [court of appeal] reasoned that chalk is not a liquid and did not
     damage the sidewalk. Therefore, it found the defendant did not violate
     the statute. (*Ibid.*)
5.   _____The Legislature subsequently amended the statute to delete the
     phrase "defaces with paint or any other liquid" and substitute in its place
     the phrase "defaces with graffiti or other inscribed material."
6.   Accordingly, the *Mackinney* case is of no assistance to appellant's cause.

. . .

   a.   Later, the legislature got rid of the phrase "defaces with paint or
        any other liquid" and replaced it with "defaces with graffiti or other
        inscribed material."
   b.   That's why *Mackinney* doesn't help appellant's case.
   c.   Appellant says he didn't violate the statute because "defacing" means
        to make a permanent mark on something, but the marks he made on
        the window could easily be wiped off.
   d.   In *Mackinney*, a court found that making chalk marks on a sidewalk
        did not deface it. Appellant says that this case is just like that one.
   e.   The court of appeal said the defendant didn't violate the statute
        because chalk is a solid, not a liquid.
   f.   Appellant admits that the other statute made it illegal to deface some-
        thing with paint or another liquid. The statute in this case does not.

**Read the case below and then complete the exercises that follow:**

5 Cal.App.4th 941, 102 Cal.Rptr.2d 511
Court of Appeal, Second District, Division 4, California.
In re NICHOLAS Y., a Person Coming Under the Juvenile Court Law.
The People, Plaintiff and Respondent,
v.
Nicholas Y., Defendant and Appellant.

Dec. 21, 2000.
. . .

EPSTEIN, Acting P.J.
Appellant Nicholas Y. appeals from [his conviction]. He contends the evidence
was insufficient to prove he violated Penal Code section 594 (vandalism). . . .

[W]e hold that writing on the glass window of a projection booth of a motion picture theater constituted defacing, and hence vandalism within the meaning of the statute. . . .

## FACTUAL SUMMARY

The evidence . . . proved that in the early morning hours of February 11, 2000, appellant wrote on a glass window of a projection booth at an A.M.C. theater with a Sharpie marker. After his arrest, appellant admitted to police that he had written "RTK" on the window. . . . Appellant said the initials stood for "The Right to Crime."

At the close of the prosecution's case, appellant's counsel argued that no defacing of or damage to property had been proved, stating: "[i]t's a piece of glass with a marker on it. You take a rag and wipe it off. End of case. It's ridiculous." The prosecutor countered that appellant trespassed and left fresh marks on the window, thus defacing the window with graffiti. The court found that appellant violated Penal Code section 594, subdivision (a), a misdemeanor.

## DISCUSSION
### I

Penal Code section 594 provides, in relevant part: "(a) Every person who maliciously commits any of the following acts with respect to any real or personal property not his or her own, in cases other than those specified by state law, is guilty of vandalism: (1) Defaces with graffiti or other inscribed material. . . . As used in this section the term 'graffiti or other inscribed material' includes any unauthorized inscription, word, figure, mark, or design that is written, marked, etched, scratched, drawn, or painted on real or personal property."

Appellant contends he did not violate the statute because the word "deface" [means] a "permanent alteration" of the surface of an object rather than the easily removed marking he placed on the window. He compares the facts of this case to chalk writing on a sidewalk held not to constitute vandalism in violation of Penal Code section 594 in *Mackinney v. Nielsen* 69 F.3d 1002 (9th Cir.1995). As appellant acknowledges, however, the statutory language interpreted in that case was different, making it "illegal to (1) *deface 'with paint or any other liquid,'* (2) damage or (3) destroy any real or personal property that is not one's own." (*Id.* at p. 1005, emphasis added.) The [court of appeal] reasoned that chalk is not a liquid and did not damage the sidewalk. Therefore, it found the defendant did not violate the statute. (*Ibid.*) The Legislature subsequently amended the statute to delete the phrase "defaces with paint or any other liquid" and substitute in its place the phrase "defaces with graffiti or other inscribed material." Accordingly, the *Mackinney* case is of no assistance to appellant's cause.

· · ·

Graffiti may be, and regularly is, created with marker pens. (See *Sherwin-Williams Co. v. City of Los Angeles* (1993) 4 Cal.4th 893, 901, 16 Cal.Rptr.2d 215, 844 P.2d 534.) It would be irrational to hold that use of a marker pen on, for example, a painted or stucco surface constitutes vandalism in violation of Penal Code section 594, subdivision (a)(1) while use of a marker pen on glass is not. Each mars the surface with graffiti, which must be removed in order to restore the original condition. This pragmatic fact is consistent with the primary meaning of the word deface as defined in the Oxford English Dictionary: "To mar the face, features, or appearance of; to spoil or ruin the figure, form, or beauty of; to disfigure.". . . This definition does not incorporate an element of permanence. Thus, it appears that a marring of the surface is no less a defacement because it is more easily removed. It follows that appellant was properly found to have violated Penal Code section 594, subdivision (a)(1).

· · ·

## DISPOSITION
For the foregoing reasons, the judgment is affirmed.

HASTINGS, and CURRY, JJ., concur.

**Answer the following questions about the case:**

1. In which court is the case being heard?
2. What decisions have been made in court about the case previously?
3. Who is the appellant in this case?
4. What is the appellant arguing in his appeal?
5. Is it important in the case that Nicholas (the defendant) was arrested at the A.M.C. theater?
6. Is it important that the marker pen he used to write on the glass was the Sharpie brand?
7. Is it important that the marks he made could easily be wiped off the glass?
8. Having read the statute (§ 594 of the California Penal Code) and the case, which particular word in the statute do you think the court must interpret in order to make its ruling on the appeal?
9. How is the *Mackinney v. Nielsen* case that is referred to relevant to the matter before the court?
10. Which party do you think wanted to rely on the *Mackinney* case? Why?
11. Why does the court decide not to rely on the decision in the *Mackinney* case?

12. What did the court hold in the *Nicholas Y.* case? What was the key reason, or reasons, for this decision?

## Exercise 3   Example of a short case about burglary (United States)

### Lead-in

Before starting this exercise, go back to the burglary exercises in chapter 1 and look at the Washington residential burglary statute. What kind of building must be entered in order to violate that statute?

**Match the terms on the left with the words or phrases on the right that mean the same thing.**

| Word or phrase | Definition |
| --- | --- |
| 1. charged with | a. purchase |
| 2. occupy | b. look for |
| 3. acquire | c. live in |
| 4. seek | d. formally accused of |

**Read the extract from the case below and answer the questions that follow:**[7]

Appellant was convicted of burglary of a dwelling house. He seeks reversal of his conviction on the ground that the building he was charged with entering was not shown to be a "dwelling house" under Alaska law. We reverse.

The offense of burglary is dealt with in Article 3 of Chapter 5 of the Alaska Criminal Code. The term "dwelling house" is defined in § 65-5-35 of the Article as follows: "A building is a 'dwelling house' if any part of it is usually occupied by any person."

Testimony showed that defendant entered an unoccupied house in Fairbanks, Alaska, on the night of December 21, 1954, and took several coats. The evidence shows that the house had not been lived in for more than a year prior to the entry. The owner, who lived not far from the place, had acquired the structure in 1952, but apparently had never lived in it himself.

1. Which of the following is a statement of the procedural history of this case?
   a. Appellant was convicted of burglary. He appeals. The court reverses his conviction.

    b.  The offense of burglary is dealt with in Article 3 of Chapter 5 of the Alaska Criminal Code.

    c.  Testimony showed that defendant entered an unoccupied house in Fairbanks, Alaska, on the night of December 21, 1954, and took several coats.

    d.  The building the defendant was charged with entering was not a "dwelling house" under Alaska law.

2.  Which of the following could be a statement of the legal issue in this case?

    a.  Article 3 of Chapter 5 of the Alaska Criminal Code.

    b.  Defendant entered an unoccupied house in Fairbanks, Alaska, on the night of December 21, 1954, and took several coats.

    c.  Is burglary a crime in Alaska?

    d.  Was the house, which had not been lived in for more than a year before defendant entered it, a "dwelling house" under Alaska law?

3.  Which of the following could be a statement of the important facts of the case?

    a.  Defendant entered an unoccupied house that had not been lived in for more than a year. He took several coats. The owner had never lived there.

    b.  § 65-5-35 of the Article states that "Any building is deemed a 'dwelling house' if any part of it is usually occupied by any person."

    c.  Appellant was convicted of burglary of a dwelling house. He seeks reversal of his conviction.

    d.  Defendant claims that the building he was charged with entering was not a "dwelling house" under Alaska law.

## Exercise 4    Interpretation of a UK statute

### Lead-in

In previous exercises, you have seen various statutes dealing with the offense of burglary. Although there are some common elements, you would have seen that each burglary offense has some things that are slightly different.

The following case relates to burglary as defined in the UK Theft Act 1968, although in this particular situation, the facts relate to a charge of rape rather than theft.

1.  What do you think the possible connection between burglary and rape may be? (You may want to refer back to the exercises in chapter 1 while answering).

2.  If somebody invited you into their house mistakenly thinking you were someone else, do you think by entering, you would be doing so without permission? Why or why not?

3.  What is the most appropriate definition of "to trespass"?
    a.  Entering or being present on property without the permission of the owner, knowing you do not have permission, or not caring.
    b.  Entering a property with the consent of the owner.
    c.  Entering a property with the intention to commit a crime.
    d.  Causing damage to a property that you have entered illegally.

4.  What is the most appropriate definition of "reckless" behavior?
    a.  Conduct that is intended to cause harm.
    b.  Actions that result in unforeseeable negative consequences.
    c.  Deliberate actions that lead to property damage.
    d.  Unjustifiable disregard for the potential risks and consequences.

**Read the case below and answer the questions that follow.**

[1972] EWCA Crim 1
Case No.: 5255/B/71

IN THE COURT OF APPEAL
CRIMINAL DIVISION

Royal Courts of Justice,
5th May 1972.

Before:
LORD JUSTICE EDMUND DAVIES
LORD JUSTICE STEPHENSON
and
MR. JUSTICE BOREHAM

---

REGINA

-v-

STEPHEN WILLIAM GEORGE COLLINS

---

MR. P. PERRINS appeared on behalf of the Appellant.
MR. F. IRWIN appeared on behalf of the Crown.
Crown Copyright ©[8]

LORD JUSTICE EDMUND DAVIES: At about 2 o'clock in the early morning of Saturday 24th July of last year, a young lady of 18 went to bed at her mother's home in Colchester. . . .

. . . [She was] in a bed which is very near the . . . window of her room. . . .

At about 3.30 or 4 o'clock she awoke and she then saw in the moonlight a vague form crouched in the open window. She was unable to remember, and this is important, whether the form was on the outside of the window sill or on that part of the sill which was inside the room, and for reasons which will later become clear, that seemingly narrow point is of crucial importance.

The young lady then realised several things: first of all that the form in the window was that of a male; secondly that he was a naked male; and thirdly that he was a naked male with an erect penis. She also saw in the moonlight that his hair was blond. She thereupon leapt to the conclusion that her boyfriend . . . was paying her [a] . . . visit. She promptly sat up in bed, and the man descended from the sill and joined her in bed and they had full sexual intercourse. But there was something about him which made her think that things were not as they usually were between her and her boyfriend. The length of his hair, his voice as they had exchanged what was described as "love talk," and other features led her to the conclusion that somehow there was something different. So she turned on the bed-side light, saw that her companion was not her boyfriend. . . .

The complainant said that she would not have agreed to intercourse if she had known that the person entering her room was not her boyfriend. But there was no suggestion of any force having been used upon her, and the intercourse which took place was undoubtedly effected with no resistance on her part.

> . . .

In the course of his testimony, Collins said that he would not have gone into the room if the girl had not knelt on the bed and beckoned him into the room . . . .

> . . .

. . . Under section 9 of the Theft Act of 1968, which renders a person guilty of burglary if he enters any building or part of a building as a trespasser and with the intention of committing rape, the entry of the accused into the building must first be proved. Well, there is no doubt about that, for it is common ground that he did enter this girl's bedroom. Secondly, it must be proved that he entered as a trespasser. We will develop that point a little later. Thirdly it must be proved that he entered as a trespasser with intent at the time of entry to commit rape therein.

> . . .

. . . In the judgment of this Court, there cannot be a conviction for entering premises "as a trespasser" within the meaning of section 9 of the Theft Act unless the person entering does so knowing that he is a trespasser and nevertheless deliberately enters, or, at the very least, is reckless as to whether or not he is entering the premises of another without the other party's consent.

Having so held, the pivotal point of this appeal is whether the Crown established that this Appellant at the moment that he entered the bedroom knew perfectly well that he was not welcome there or, being reckless as to whether he was welcome or not, was nevertheless determined to enter.

That in turn involves consideration as to where he was at the time that the complainant indicated that she was welcoming him into her bedroom. . . .

. . .

. . . If she in fact appeared to be welcoming him, the Crown do not suggest that he should have realised or even suspected that she was so behaving because, despite the moonlight, she thought he was someone else. Unless the jury were entirely satisfied that the Appellant made an effective and substantial entry into the bedroom without the complainant doing or saying anything to cause him to believe that she was consenting to his entering it, he ought not to be convicted of the offence charged. . . .

. . .

We have to say that this appeal must be allowed on the basis that the jury were never invited to consider the vital question as to whether this young man did enter the premises as a trespasser, that is to say knowing perfectly well that he had no invitation to enter or reckless of whether or not his entry was with permission. . . . For the reasons we have stated, the outcome of the appeal is that this young man must be acquitted of the charge preferred against him. The appeal is accordingly allowed and his conviction quashed.

**Mark the following statements True (T) or False (F):**

1. The defendant was convicted of burglary with intent to commit rape at his original trial. **T / F**
2. The appeal rested on whether or not the defendant had entered the girl's bedroom legally or illegally. **T / F**
3. The defendant claimed he entered the bedroom and then the girl waved him to come toward her. **T / F**
4. To be a trespasser under s.9(1)(a) Theft Act 1968, a person must enter with the knowledge that he is trespassing. Any other state of mind is insufficient for the offense. **T / F**
5. The Court of Appeal found that it was possible that the defendant had only entered after having been invited by the girl and that, therefore, the original trial judge had misdirected the jury as to the meaning of "trespass" and "enter." **T / F**

**Choose the response that best answers the questions below:**

1.  Which statement best summarizes the procedural history of the case?
    a.  The defendant was found guilty of burglary with intent to commit rape at first instance. He appealed his conviction to the Court of Appeal. The Court of Appeal allowed the appeal and quashed his conviction.
    b.  The defendant was found not guilty of burglary with intent to commit rape at first instance. The prosecution appealed and the Court of Appeal accepted the appeal for a retrial.
    c.  The court of first instance found the defendant not guilty of rape.
    d.  The defendant was found guilty of rape at his original trial. His appeal was dismissed by the Court of Appeal.
2.  Which statement best summarizes the principal legal issue of the case?
    a.  Whether or not a rape can occur if consent is given by mistake.
    b.  The correct interpretation of the words "trespass" and "entry" under the 1968 Theft Act.
    c.  Whether there can be burglary without theft.
    d.  The requisite mens rea of rape.

## Exercise 5    Another example of the interpretation of a UK statute

### Lead-in

In the previous case (exercise 4), you saw how the court interpreted the meaning of "trespasser" under the UK Theft Act 1968. The case below also concerns burglary under the Theft Act, but you will see that the issue is different.

**Match the following words (which appear commonly in cases) with the correct definition:**

| Word | Definition |
|---|---|
| 1. convicted | a. the punishment given to someone who has been convicted of a crime |
| 2. sentence | b. an illegal act; a crime |
| 3. compensation | c. money or something else that is given to make up for harm, damage, or loss caused by someone's actions |
| 4. offence (UK)/offense (US) | d. found guilty of a crime by a court of law |

**Read the case below and answer the questions that follow:**

[1985] EWCA Crim 3

Case No.: 3341/B2/84
IN THE COURT OF APPEAL
CRIMINAL DIVISION
Royal Courts of Justice,
18th January 1985

—————

REGINA
-v-
VINCENT EDWARD PATRICK BROWN

—————

. . .

Crown copyright ©[9]

LORD JUSTICE WATKINS: On 18th May 1984 the appellant, now 24 years of age, in the Crown Court at Luton, before his Honour Judge Colston and a jury, was convicted of two offences of burglary and sentenced by a fine of £50 upon each count. He was ordered to pay compensation of £80.97. He appeals against his conviction.

The facts were that just after midnight on 27th November 1983 Mr. McLean, who lives in Watford Way, Hendon, heard the sound of breaking glass outside. He looked out and on the other side of the road observed two men at a shop known as "Argos." The first of them was a man called Peerless. He pleaded guilty to the two offences of burglary I have mentioned. The second of them was alleged to be the appellant. The second man, the appellant, was, Mr. McLean said, partially inside the shop front display. The top half of him was inside and he was rummaging about. Mr. McLean said: "I assumed his feet were on the ground." He was partly obscured by the other man. Mr. McLean asked the lady who was with him to dial 999, and she did so. He spoke on the telephone to someone for a few minutes and then he again looked across the road. He saw the men putting property into a black bag. They then walked off . . . . [T]he police made their appearance on the scene having been called there by the telephone message to which I have already referred.

The appellant was arrested on the spot. . . .

The appellant and Peerless were charged with stealing a briefcase and a gentleman's travel set and the theft of an electric razor. This was found on

Peerless after he was arrested. The prosecution's case in part was that the two men had taken these goods from the window display of Argos. . . .

Section 9(1) of the Theft Act 1968, so far as material, provides: "(1) A person is guilty of burglary if (a) he enters any building . . . as a trespasser and with intent to commit any such offence as is mentioned in subsection (2) below . . ." and that, I should add for the sake of completeness, includes the offence of theft.

Mr. Richardson [for the appellant] contends that there can be no offence committed under the provisions of section 9(1) unless the person, accused of burglary, is found upon the facts to have been at the relevant time wholly within the building. It is insufficient, he says, for conviction that any part of the body of the accused be outside the building at that time. . . . Mr. Richardson also prays in aid what was said by this court in the case of *R. v. Parkin* (1951) 34 Cr.App.R. 1. That was a case in which the court had to construe section 28(4) of the Larceny Act 1916. . . . That subsection, so far as relevant, reads: "Every person who shall be found by night . . . (4) in any building with intent to commit any felony therein; shall be guilty of a misdemeanour . . .". The facts which the court had to consider were that the appellant was found by night halfway up some piping at the side of a building. He was seen by a police officer to have one of his hands through a window for the purpose of pulling himself inside.

Mr. Justice Lynskey, in giving the judgment of the court, said: "We have to construe this sub-section according to its clear words. . . . The ordinary meaning of the English words as applied to the circumstances of this case is that the appellant was not found in the building but was found outside the building, trying to get into it." It would be very surprising, so it seems to us, if that court had come to any different conclusion having regard to the precise words of subsection (4) which, I repeat, for essential purposes were "be found in any building." One can easily appreciate that in order to be found in any building you would have to be totally within it. Those are not the words, however, which appear in the subsection which is now for us to construe.

. . .

[T]he offence cannot be committed unless the entry has been made by one who was a trespasser. However, it seems to me to be a ridiculous proposition that a person can go along the street, break a shop window, put his hand within and steal goods and not be held to have entered the shop as a trespasser. As we see it, it is a question of fact for the jury as to whether or not there has been an entry for the purpose of section 9(1). We believe a jury should be directed that there should be an effective entry before a conviction can be made under this subsection. In this case, although he did not in terms use the word "effective," the judge's direction to the jury helped them as well as any jury could properly be assisted having regard to the facts of the case. We find that his illustrations as what could amount to an entry are wholly appropriate, that is to say that having broken a window, to put a hand, an arm or the upper part of a body through a broken shop window is capable of being found to be an entry.

It is unnecessary to say more than that according to the facts of the case the jury must be left to decide, directed in the ways in which we have suggested, as to whether or not there has been an entry. There was clearly in this case an entry as a trespasser. The jury properly so found and were adequately and suitably directed for that purpose. The appeal is therefore dismissed.

**Answer the following questions:**

1.   What was the decision of the court in this case at the original trial?
2.   Who has appealed the case to the Court of Appeal?
3.   What do you think were the most important fact(s) reported by the witness, Mr. McLean?
4.   Why did the appellant refer to the case of *R. v. Parkin* in his defense?
5.   Why did the court say the *Parkin* case was not relevant to the appeal (i.e., it "distinguished" that case)?
6.   What do you think was the key issue that the Court of Appeal had to decide?
7.   What reason(s) did the court use to base its decision on the appeal?

## Exercise 6    Example of a US civil law case

### Lead-in

Imagine that a dolphin is held in an aquarium in the Northern Territory of Australia. A group of activists believes that keeping a dolphin in captivity is cruel because they are such intelligent creatures. Assume that they sue the aquarium under the Animal Protection Act 2018 sections that you examined in chapter 1. Based only on those statutes, how would you answer the following questions?

1.   What if the aquarium owner could show that they provide high living standards compared to similar aquariums? Would the plaintiffs lose?
2.   What would happen if the defendant is found liable under the Act? What remedy do you think a court would provide?
3.   Who would the court give the remedy to?

## Some common words and phrases in case opinions

The opinion that you are about to read contains quite a few words and phrases that you may come across in other cases. Some of them are in the column on the left.

**Match each word or phrase on the left with the phrase on the right that explains or defines it:**

| Word or phrase | Definition |
| --- | --- |
| 1. does not lie | a. does not exist |
| 2. governed | b. the right to sue |
| 3. well settled | c. something the court gives a party to help it |
| 4. writ | d. determined by or controlled by |
| 5. contention | e. generally agreed upon by all authorities |
| 6. petition | f. an official request to the court |
| 7. standing | g. a point of view stated in an argument |
| 8. relief | h. a written command by a court |

**Now, use four of the words in the column on the left to complete the passage below:**

Defendant appeals from the judgment of the trial court finding him guilty of vandalism. His _______ is that he did not violate the statute because he made marks that could be easily removed. However, it is _______ that a person can commit vandalism by making easily removable marks. This case is _______ by Nicholas Y. In that case, the marks that defendant made on a piece of glass with a marker were quickly wiped off. Nevertheless, they were held to deface the surface. Accordingly, we cannot grant defendant any _______.

**Read the case below and answer the questions that follow.**

124 A.D.3d 1334

999 N.Y.S.2d 652

In the Matter of the NONHUMAN RIGHTS PROJECT, INC.,
on behalf of KIKO, Petitioner–Appellant,

v.

Carmen PRESTI, Individually and as an Officer and Director of the
Primate Sanctuary, Inc., Christie E. Presti, Individually and as an Officer
and Director of the Primate Sanctuary, Inc. and the Primate Sanctuary, Inc.,
Respondents–Respondents.

Supreme Court[10]
Appellate Division, Fourth Department, New York.
Jan. 2, 2015
PRESENT: SMITH, J.P., PERADOTTO, LINDLEY, VALENTINO, and WHALEN, JJ. MEMORANDUM:

Petitioner, an organization seeking better treatment and housing of, inter alia, nonhuman primates, commenced this proceeding seeking a writ of habeas corpus on behalf of Kiko, a chimpanzee. Rather than seeking Kiko's immediate release, however, the petition alleges that Kiko is illegally confined because he is kept in unsuitable conditions, and it seeks to have Kiko's confinement transferred to a different facility selected by The North American Primate Sanctuary Alliance. On appeal from a judgment dismissing the petition, petitioner contends that Kiko is entitled to the relief sought. Contrary to petitioner's contention, we conclude that Supreme Court properly dismissed the petition.

Regardless of whether we agree with petitioner's claim that Kiko is a person within the statutory and common-law definition of the writ, " 'habeas corpus relief nonetheless is unavailable as [that] claim . . ., even if meritorious, would not entitle [Kiko] to immediate release' " (*People ex rel. Gonzalez v. Wayne County Sheriff,* 96 A.D.3d 1698, 1699, 947 N.Y.S.2d 738, lv. denied 21 N.Y.3d 852, 2013 WL 1760829; see *People ex rel. Shannon v. Khahaifa,* 74 A.D.3d 1867, 1867, 901 N.Y.S.2d 883, lv. dismissed 15 N.Y.3d 868, 910 N.Y.S.2d 34, 936 N.E.2d 916; *People ex rel. Hall v. Rock,* 71 A.D.3d 1303, 1304, 895 N.Y.S.2d 889, appeal dismissed 14 N.Y.3d 882, 903 N.Y.S.2d 338, 929 N.E.2d 401, lv. denied 15 N.Y.3d 703, 2010 WL 2605955). It is well settled that a habeas corpus proceeding must be dismissed where the subject of the petition is not entitled to immediate release from custody (see *People ex rel. Kaplan v. Commissioner of Correction of City of N.Y.,* 60 N.Y.2d 648, 649, 467 N.Y.S.2d 566, 454 N.E.2d 1309; *People ex rel. Douglas v. Vincent,* 50 N.Y.2d 901, 903, 431 N.Y.S.2d 518, 409 N.E.2d 990). Here, petitioner does not seek Kiko's immediate release, nor does petitioner allege that Kiko's continued detention is unlawful. Rather, petitioner seeks to have Kiko placed in a different facility that petitioner deems more appropriate. Consequently, even assuming, for the sake of argument, that we agreed with petitioner that Kiko should be deemed a person for the purpose of this application, and further assuming, arguendo, that petitioner has standing to commence this proceeding on behalf of Kiko, this matter is governed by the line of cases standing for the proposition that habeas corpus does not lie where a petitioner seeks only to change the conditions of confinement rather than the confinement itself (see generally *People ex rel. Dawson v.*

*Smith*, 69 N.Y.2d 689, 690–691, 512 N.Y.S.2d 19, 504 N.E.2d 386; *Matter of Berrian v. Duncan*, 289 A.D.2d 655, 655, 733 N.Y.S.2d 790; *People ex rel. McCallister v. McGinnis*, 251 A.D.2d 835, 835, 673 N.Y.S.2d 946). We therefore conclude that habeas corpus does not lie herein.

It is hereby ORDERED that the judgment so appealed from is unanimously affirmed without costs.

**Mark the following statements as True (T) or False (F):**

1.  The court applies the statutory definition of the writ of habeas corpus, not the common law definition. **T / F**
2.  The plaintiff wants Kiko the chimpanzee to be moved to a place where conditions would be more suitable for him. **T / F**
3.  The court does not decide whether the Nonhuman Rights Project has standing to represent Kiko. **T / F**
4.  The Appellate Division of the Supreme Court decides that Kiko is not a "person" under New York law. **T / F**

**Answer the following questions using full sentences:**

1.  Based on the court's discussion, what do you think a writ of habeas corpus is generally used for?
2.  Did the Appellate Division grant plaintiff's petition for a writ of habeas corpus? Explain the court's reasoning for its decision.
3.  Imagine a situation where all of the facts are the same as in this case, except that the petitioner is a human being who wants to be transferred from a prison with poor conditions to one with better conditions. Would the outcome of the case be any different?
4.  Explain what, if anything, the Nonhuman Rights Project was trying to achieve for nonhuman primates in general by filing this action.

## Exercise 7   Practicing drafting case briefs

You may have noticed that by completing the exercises on the previous example cases, you have basically been working out the kinds of details you would need to draft a "case brief" (you can refer back to the introduction for a brief explanation of a case brief). You now have a chance to practice this skill, which will be very useful to you during your legal studies. Different LL.M. or other law programs may have slightly differing ways in which they may want students to put together case briefs. However, almost all will require the details that are asked below.

You will find a number of cases reprinted in chapter 3 (for example, *In re NICHOLAS Y* on page 60).

Read the *Nicholas Y.* case and then review the model case brief for it below.

## Citation

In re NICHOLAS Y. 85 Cal.App.4th 941 (2000)

## Procedural History

California Court of Appeal
Nicholas Y., appellant, People of CA, respondent. Appellant was found guilty of vandalism. He appeals. He contends there was insufficient evidence of vandalism because there was no proof that he "defaced" the window. Affirmed. (Appeal dismissed.)

## Facts

After his arrest, appellant admitted to police that he had written on a glass window of a projection booth at a movie theater with a marker. The marks on the glass could be easily removed.

## Issue

Did Nicholas "deface" the glass window when he made easily removable marks on it?

## Holding

Yes. Even easily removable marks still "deface" a surface.

## Reasoning

Cal. Penal Code section 594 says that anyone who "defaces with graffiti or other inscribed material" commits vandalism, but the plain meaning of the word "deface" does not include the idea of "permanence." Marks made on any surfaces must be removed to restore them to their original condition, so it would be irrational to say that marks on only some surfaces are graffiti. It would not make sense to say some marks are graffiti and some are not, based on how hard they are to remove.

Now choose some of the other cases reprinted in chapter 3 and practice writing some case briefs using the following headings:

Citation
Procedural history
Facts
Issue
Holding
Reasoning

## Conclusion

Hopefully you have worked your way through the exercises in this chapter and produced some case briefs. You can look at some of the model answers for briefs in the appendix to compare. By doing these things, you will have practiced the following:

- Identifying the key legal concepts and principles of a point of law from reading a case (also known as an "opinion").
- Identifying the structure of a case, including the procedural history, case facts, legal issues, decision, and reasoning.
- Recognizing and comprehending specialized legal terminology commonly used in common law case law.
- Constructing a case brief with its necessary structural components (procedural history, case facts, legal issues, decision, and reasoning).

If you can put together a good-quality case brief, you will have demonstrated your ability to read a case effectively. You will also be very well set up to move on to the next chapter of the book, in which we start writing answers to legal problems using a particular structure.

*Chapter 3*
# Legal Writing—(C)IRAC

So far, we have concentrated on some very important reading skills that all law students need in order to be successful in their studies. You have also used the exercises on cases in chapter 2 to write some case briefs, which will be invaluable in managing the demands of learning the law. When completing the exercises on statutes and cases, you have had to use your critical thinking and analytical skills to answer the questions. Putting together case briefs has also required you to be able to identify the key facts of a case and to distill the decision and reasoning of the court into a short, easy-to-understand summary. This chapter will now build on the skills you have developed to produce written answers to legal questions.

While common law lawyers are often (rightly) characterized in popular culture as being highly skilled in oral arguments, both law students and lawyers also need to have very good writing skills. While there are many different forms of legal writing, it would be fair to say that most of these forms share an underlying objective of being *persuasive*. In other words, they are written to persuade the court, a client, or an opponent's lawyers that what you are writing is correct and should be accepted or followed. Moreover, these different forms mostly share some common characteristics. Specifically, legal writing tends to take general principles of law and apply them to particular factual scenarios. This involves some sort of analysis of the facts of a particular case (which will require establishing the important/relevant details of the matter); identification of the law that applies to the case (which will come from statutes, cases, and most likely a combination of both); and then an application of those general principles of law to the specific facts to answer a legal problem or provide legal advice (in effect, the "answer").[1] With the possible exception of academics studying and writing about legal theory, most lawyers in practice and law students will find themselves producing writing that follows this pattern of going from general principles to specific advice/answers.

## IRAC

In order to support you in developing your legal writing skills, this chapter will introduce you to a structure for putting together written answers to legal problems called "IRAC" (we will deal with the "(C)" in the title of this chapter a bit later). While this is a structure used mostly by law students when answering problems they are given during their studies and in exams, as you progress in your legal careers you will see that iterations of the IRAC structure are helpful in producing lots of different types of legal writing, from memoranda of advice for clients to briefs written for court proceedings. Therefore, once you have mastered thinking and writing in an IRAC structure, you will find it very useful throughout your legal careers.

At this point, we should quickly explain what "IRAC" means. In fact, IRAC is an acronym, standing for Issue, Rule, Analysis, and Conclusion.[2] Before explaining what these words mean in this context, we should also point out that you may come across other variations of IRAC, for example, CRAC (Conclusion, Rule, Analysis/Application, and Conclusion) or CREAC (Conclusion, Rule, Explanation, Application, and Conclusion). We will not cover the particular differences in these other structures since they are, in essence, broadly very similar to IRAC. You may find that if you go to law school, one of these other structures is preferred. However, if you can use IRAC effectively, you should have no problem adjusting to a similar structure.

Let's look briefly at each of the components of IRAC:

*Issue* This is effectively the legal issue in question. It may be expressed as a question, or alternatively, you may need to read the problem given to you in order to work out the issue. In the latter case, it is very important that you correctly identify the key issue. (You will need to go through a similar process as when you identify the legal issue in a case brief—see chapter 2.) As you progress with your studies, the problems you encounter will become more complex, and you may have to address multiple issues in your response.

***Rule*** This refers to the general legal principles that are relevant to the legal issue that needs to be addressed in the problem. The law may come from statutes and/or cases and, depending on the complexity of the problem, may involve multiple points of law.

***Analysis*** This section of your written response will typically be the most detailed. In this part, you will apply the legal principles that you set out in the Rule section to the specific facts of the problem you are addressing.

***Conclusion*** In this section, you will effectively give the answer to the legal problem in light of the analysis you have completed.

Although an IRAC response follows this specific structure, it is unusual (and unnecessary) to use individual subheadings (Issue, Rule, etc.). However, structuring your paragraph or essay using IRAC is an effective and relatively easy way to write in a clear and persuasive manner. If you recall, we noted above that the objective of a great deal of legal writing is to persuade the reader of the force of your points. IRAC is a good way of organizing your ideas to do this.

At this point, it is probably worth pointing out that the writing culture in common law countries may be different from the culture you are familiar with. It is considered good practice in the English-speaking world, for example, to be direct and clear when you are writing. This is why professors in common law countries put a lot of emphasis on structure and setting out the key points as clearly as possible, so that the reader is left with no doubt about what the writer intends to say. We call this a "writer-responsible" culture.[3] In contrast, there are other writing cultures (characterized as "reader-responsible") where ambiguity and an implicit approach are not just tolerated but seen as features of good-quality academic writing. Students from these cultures may find it difficult to adapt to structures such as IRAC. They may even think that this attempt to be clear patronizes the reader because it often repeats basic things and seems to want to "hold the reader's hand." In emphasizing the effectiveness of the IRAC structure, we do not mean to imply that "writer-responsible" cultures are necessarily superior. However, on the assumption that you are using this book to help acculturate yourself into common law ways of thinking (for example, to study for an LL.M. in a US university), you may find it beneficial to try to adopt a "writer-responsible" approach. IRAC will help you to do this.

In addition, it is very challenging to learn how to write anything just by reading a book or a chapter about it. Just as people don't tend to learn how to drive by reading a manual, students generally learn best when they write under supervision, receive lots of feedback, and do a lot of practice. If you are using this book for self-study, you may find trying to teach yourself IRAC quite frustrating and difficult. We include some additional references at the end of this book, which include some useful texts on writing. You will also find some model answers to some of the exercises in this chapter. However, if you find yourself really struggling with IRAC, you may need to reach out to people to help you. University writing centers, for example, may be able to support you.

## More complex problems that have multiple issues

The exercises in this workbook will be relatively simple from a legal perspective. However, during your legal studies and career, it is almost certainly the case that the writing you will do will relate to matters that have multiple, complex issues. In such cases, it is often preferable to structure your response using IRAC for each separate issue. You may then have a final, concluding sentence that gives an overall answer. The example IRAC response below uses this structure so that you can get an idea of how this might look.

## Topic sentences—turning IRAC into CIRAC or CRAC

Finally, before we look at an example of an IRAC paragraph, we will draw your attention to one further way of making your writing clear: using a topic sentence at the start of your answer. A topic sentence contains the main idea of your writing, such that the reader can understand immediately what you are arguing in the subsequent text. In other words, if you are answering a legal problem, the topic sentence will contain the brief answer to the question. Opinions may differ about using a topic sentence to start an IRAC response, which in essence turns it into a CIRAC or CRAC response. It may be that professors at your law school do not want you to start with a topic sentence. If that is the case, you should do what they advise. However, we feel using topic sentences in this way is a very effective strategy for making your writing clear from the start. It will also help you to keep your focus on writing persuasive arguments justifying the answer to the question. There will be an opportunity to practice topic sentences in some of the exercises below, if you wish to do so.

## Example of an (C)IRAC answer

Read the question and response below and see if you can identify the different parts of the IRAC structure.

Read the situation below and write a paragraph using the IRAC structure in order to answer the question:

*Sally and Stewart have been married for 25 years, but Stewart forgot their wedding anniversary. The day after, Stewart gave Sally this note: "In consideration of 25 years of marriage, my dearest, I will buy you a million-dollar diamond pendant." Sally took this very seriously, and, when Stewart failed to give her the pendant, filed for divorce and commenced court proceedings to enforce his promise about the pendant. Part of Stewart's defense is that the value of the claim is excessive. In other words, what Sally provided him was not worth a million-dollar pendant.*

What is the likely outcome of this matter? (For the purposes of answering, assume the only legal point at issue concerns consideration [defined as the mutual exchange of something of value, which is a required element of a common law contract]).

A student was provided with some cases that are relevant to this problem and drafted the answer below (which includes a topic sentence at the start):

*It is unlikely Sally would be able to enforce any agreement with Stewart owing to the fact that the consideration has already been provided, even if the court would not interfere with the amount claimed. There are two issues in the case. The first issue is whether consideration (in this case love and affection given over the previous 25 years) can be valid in respect of a promise that has only just been made. It is established law that any service already performed as part of a voluntary promise cannot later qualify as consideration to validate a contract* Harrington v. Taylor, *225 N.C. 690, 36 S.E.2d 2 (1945). Any moral obligation that Stewart has to compensate Sally for her love and affection cannot on its own be adequate consideration to enforce a contract* Lewis v. Hester, *225 N.C.App. 83 (2014). There is also a presumption that services performed by one member of the family for another, within the unity of the family, are presumed to have been rendered in obedience to a moral obligation and without expectation of compensation* Id. *In this case, Sally has already provided the services voluntarily without expectation that Stewart would exchange something in value for it. Therefore, having provided the service, Sally cannot subsequently claim payment under a contract because no contract can exist without consideration. She had already provided the service freely before claiming she should be compensated. In conclusion, it is likely the court would find there was not an enforceable contract owing to this not constituting valid consideration.*

*The second issue is whether the value of the consideration is relevant to any decision made by the court. It is established law that the courts will not interfere or try to correct a bad bargain agreed by parties. Consideration does not have to match or be adequate* Hejl v. Hood, Hargett & Associates, Inc., *674 S.E.2d 425, 196 N.C.App. 299 (N.C. App. 2009). In this case, the fact that Stewart was the one who made the initial "offer" of a pendant worth $1,000,000 would, in any event, undermine his claim that the value of Sally's claim is excessive. Still, the value of consideration does not have to be adequate, and so he could not mount a legal argument that the services provided by Sally were not worth this amount. Therefore, if the court did conclude that there was a contract between the parties, it would not seek to rule on the amount of the consideration since parties are free to decide themselves what should be exchanged.*

*In conclusion, it is likely the court would find there was not an enforceable contract owing to a lack of valid consideration. However, if the court did rule there was a contract, the court would not seek to interfere with the amount claimed, even if it seemed excessive.*

Let's analyze the different parts of this student's answer:

*It is unlikely Sally would be able to enforce any agreement with Stewart owing to the fact that the consideration has already been provided, even if the court would not interfere with the amount claimed.*

This is a topic sentence, setting out clearly what the writer will argue in their response to the question. If you add one, it effectively changes the response from an IRAC structure to CIRAC or CRAC. As we noted before, while there are good reasons to add a topic sentence, it will very much depend on what your professors prefer, so make sure you check with them if you want to add a topic sentence.

*There are two issues in the case. The first issue is whether consideration (in this case love and affection given over the previous 25 years) can be valid in respect of a promise that has only just been made.*

The writer has analyzed the question and identified two legal issues. In order to deal with each issue more clearly, they have chosen to state and analyze the first issue separately. This is very likely what your professors at law school will prefer.

*It is established law that any service already performed as part of a voluntary promise cannot later qualify as consideration to validate a contract* Harrington v. Taylor, *225 N.C. 690, 36 S.E.2d 2 (1945). Any moral obligation that Stewart has to compensate Sally for her love and affection cannot on its own be adequate consideration to enforce a contract* Lewis v. Hester, *225 N.C.App. 83 (2014). There is also a presumption that services performed by one member of the family for another, within the unity of the family, are presumed to have been rendered in obedience to a moral obligation and without expectation of compensation* Id.

In respect of the first issue, the writer then gives the "Rule," in other words, the relevant law relating to the issue identified. In this case, the law comes from cases rather than a statute. You will also notice that citations are given to the sources of law. This is to enable a reader to check the stated law for themselves.

*In this case, Sally has already provided the services voluntarily without expectation that Stewart would exchange something in value for it. Therefore, having provided the service, Sally cannot subsequently claim payment under a contract because no contract can exist without consideration. She had already provided the service freely before claiming she should be compensated.*

In this part of the response, the writer is applying the law in respect of the first issue to the particular set of facts of the question. This is the "Analysis" section of the IRAC response. Since the issues and law in this regard are quite simple, the analysis section in this example is short and does not need to cross-refer to the cases again. However, as questions get more complex, the analysis part will become much longer, and it will almost certainly be necessary to refer back to specific statutes and/or cases.

*In conclusion, it is likely the court would find there was not an enforceable contract owing to this not constituting valid consideration.*

Lastly, the writer gives their conclusion to the analysis of the first issue.

*The second issue is whether the value of the consideration is relevant to any decision made by the court.*

Having dealt with the first issue, the writer now defines the second issue that needs to be considered.

*It is established law that the courts will not interfere or try to correct a bad bargain agreed by parties. Consideration does not have to match or be adequate* Hejl v. Hood, Hargett & Associates, Inc., *674 S.E.2d 425, 196 N.C.App. 299 (N.C. App. 2009).*

With regard to the second issue, the writer states the applicable rule.

*In this case, the fact that Stewart was the one who made the initial "offer" of a pendant worth $1,000,000 would, in any event, undermine his claim that the value of Sally's claim is excessive. In any event, the value of consideration does not have to be adequate, and so he could not mount a legal argument that the services provided by Sally were not worth this amount.*

The writer then applies the law to the set of facts in the question, which for the second issue relates to whether consideration needs to be adequate or equal.

*Therefore, if the court did conclude that there was a contract between the parties, it would not seek to rule on the amount of the consideration since parties are free to decide themselves what should be exchanged.*

Having analyzed the second issue, the writer concludes by setting out the answer to this part of the question.

*In conclusion, it is likely the court would find there was not an enforceable contract owing to a lack of valid consideration. However, if the court did rule there was a contract, the court would not seek to interfere with the amount claimed, even if it seemed excessive.*

Finally, the writer makes a general conclusion, answering the question by summarizing the responses to both issues. You will also note that it is effectively repeating in large part the ideas set out in the topic sentence. From a structural perspective, the writer has stated in brief the answer to the question using a topic sentence, then gone through the various stages of analysis, then repeated the answer at the end. This is an effective way of making your overall point very clear, which helps it to be more persuasive. As we have noted, this slightly changes the structure of the response from IRAC to CIRAC or CRAC. However, the overall way of analyzing the question and responding to it remains much the same. If you can write effectively in an IRAC structure, you can also do it for CIRAC, CRAC, or whatever other similar structure you may be asked to produce during your studies.

Before you start looking at the exercises in this chapter, we will briefly mention outlining. An outline is a plan for your writing and functions as a sort of roadmap. Students sometimes think they do not have enough time (particularly in exams) to write outlines. However, we think planning your work is a very good discipline. If English is not your first language, it is especially important. During the outlining process, you can think deeply about the legal issues, and the statutes and cases you will need to use to address them, without having to worry too much about grammar and other language problems. Once you have an outline, the "intellectual" part of putting together the paragraph or essay has been done. When you write the answer using your outline, you can then focus on getting the language right, which will make the overall product better—and probably increase your grade.

There are no strict rules on how to put together an outline, but we give below an example of one that you could use to answer the *Sally and Stewart* question we have just looked at.

> <u>Topic sentence:</u>* It is unlikely Sally would be able to enforce any agreement with Stewart owing to the fact that the consideration has already been provided, even if the court would not interfere with the amount claimed.
>
> <u>Issue:</u> Two issues—(1) is the consideration valid; (2) is adequacy of the consideration a factor.
>
> <u>Rule for issue 1:</u> service already performed, cannot be a consideration (Harrington case); moral obligation not enough (Lewis case); presumption of no contract in a social and domestic scenario (Lewis case again).
>
> <u>Analysis issue 1:</u> Sally already provided the service freely.
>
> <u>Conclusion for issue 1:</u> no consideration, therefore not enforceable.
>
> <u>Rule for issue 2:</u> consideration doesn't need to match or be adequate (Hejl case).
>
> <u>Analysis:</u> adequacy not needed, and anyway, Stewart offered the necklace worth $1 million.
>
> <u>Conclusion for issue 2:</u> Stewart's argument won't work if there is a contract.
>
> <u>Overall conclusion:</u> no contract because no consideration; if there is a contract, adequacy not an issue.

---

*If you choose to use one, it is good practice to complete the outline first, then come back afterwards to fill in the topic sentence.

Obviously, in this example, the facts and law were relatively simple, so the outline is nearly as long as the paragraph! However, where there are multiple and complex issues and facts, using this outline structure to map out the possible answer can really help you break down the task into more manageable chunks. This will often result in you writing a much better paragraph or essay. Therefore, we recommend that you experiment with outlining in the exercises you will find in this chapter.

For the remainder of this chapter, you will work through various exercises that are designed to support you in constructing IRAC-style responses to legal questions. In time, you should be able to take any legal problem and structure your answer using IRAC. As you pursue your legal studies and career, you should see that this way of putting together a legal argument is a very effective way for a lawyer to write.

By working through all the exercises in this chapter, you should hopefully be able to do the following:

- Identify each component of the IRAC structure (and/or one of its variants) in a written legal response.
- Identify and analyze the key legal issue(s) presented in a hypothetical scenario.
- Identify relevant statutes and/or cases to address the legal issue in a hypothetical scenario.
- Apply legal principles to the facts of a hypothetical scenario.
- Incorporate references to statutes and/or cases in written answers to legal problems using an IRAC-style structure.
- Construct a coherent and accurately written response to a legal problem using appropriate legal terminology in an IRAC-style structure.

## Before you start

Many of the following exercises contain a number of questions to help guide you toward completing a full IRAC answer to the hypothetical scenarios, or "hypos," included. You may choose to use these as a way of focusing on some of the key issues and the relevant applicable law before attempting to respond to the question in the hypo. Alternatively, if you would like to go directly to answering the hypo using the IRAC format, simply ignore the guiding questions. If after starting an IRAC response you find the exercise too difficult, you can always go back to the questions as a way of getting some help.

Remember, it might be helpful to prepare an outline before you start writing the answer. Good luck!

## Exercise 1    Breach of contract[4]

### Lead-in

Most of the statutes and cases in this book have focused on elements of criminal law (the reasons for this are explained in the Introduction). The materials in this exercise, however, relate to contract law. The most basic definition of a contract is that it is an agreement between different parties that is enforceable by the court. In other words, if someone does not fulfill any of their obligations in the agreement (known as a "breach" of the contract), the party who has suffered the breach may apply to the court for a remedy.

First, consider the following questions:

1.  Why do you think people need contracts?
2.  Do you think that if a party has breached a contract, the other party has a right to end the contract? What if the breach is relatively minor?

**Complete the sentences below using words from the box.**

| | | | |
|---|---|---|---|
| terminate | term | perform | party |
| | breach | material | |

1.  This _______ of the contract states that the buyer is responsible for shipping costs.
2.  The seller will _______ all necessary repairs within two weeks.
3.  If each _______ to the contract decides to _______ the agreement, it will come to an end after one month.
4.  The seller failed to deliver the goods within the contractual deadline. This _______ resulted in legal action being taken by the buyer.
5.  The customer argued that the breach was _______. In other words, it was so important that they should have the right to end the contract.

Read the following law from the fictional jurisdiction of Collody and the exercises that follow. Then, read the hypo and answer the question given using any variation on the IRAC form.

## Collody legal authorities

## Statutes

*Collody Civil Code section 8. Breach of contract:*

(1)  A party breaches a contract if it fails to perform any term of a contract, written or oral, without a legitimate legal excuse.
(2)  Any party that breaches a contract may be liable for all foreseeable harm caused by the breach.

*Collody Civil Code section 9. Materiality of breach:*

(1)  The non-breaching party may only terminate a contract if a breach is material.
(2)  Breach is material if it either:
    a.  deprives the non-breaching party of the benefit that the contract is supposed to provide, or;
    b.  shows that the breaching party is not competent to continue doing the work described in the contract.
(3)  When a breach is only minor, the breaching party must be allowed to complete performance of its duties under the contract.

## Case summaries

### Ali's Sporting Goods v. Holmes Inc., 6 Cdy. 555 (1988)

Ali's Sporting Goods store ordered volleyballs from its supplier, Holmes, but received basketballs instead. When Ali's switched suppliers, Holmes sued for breach of contract. The court of appeal held that the breach was material and that Ali's had the right to terminate the contract. Interpreting Civil Code Section 9(1)a, the court explained that "the non-breaching party lost the benefit that the contract was supposed to provide when it received something substantially different from what the contract specified."

### Bob's Builders v. Ralph, 8 Cdy. 987 (2004)

Construction firm Bob's Builders ended its contract with subcontractor Ralph, and Ralph sued for breach of contract. The reason for Bob's Builders' action was that Ralph was three hours late in delivering a batch of concrete to Bob's Builders' construction project. The court of appeal held that Ralph had breached its contract with Bob's Builders. However, the court also held that the breach was not material. Because the breach was only minor, Bob's Builders was itself guilty of breach of contract when it ended its contract with Ralph. Although Bob's Builders had no right to end the contract, they did have the right to compensation for any damages caused by the late arrival of the concrete.

**Mark the following statements as True (T) or False (F):**

1.  Under Collody Civil Code sections 8 and 9, whenever one party breaches a contract, the other party may terminate that contract. **T / F**
2.  A material breach is one that is made without providing a legitimate legal excuse to the non-breaching party. **T / F**
3.  If a painter used interior paint on the exterior of a building because he didn't know any better, the breach would probably be material under Civil Code section 9, subsection (2)b. **T / F**
4.  Collody case law makes it clear that, even if a breach is not material, the non-breaching party may be able to recover damages from the breaching party. **T / F**

**Think about the following questions:**

1.  What is the danger to a non-breaching party if it terminates a contract in response to a breach that is not material? What part of the statute is relevant to this question? Which case would you cite?
2.  In *Ali's Sporting Goods*, the court found that the shipment of the wrong kind of ball was a material breach. What if the seller had sent the right kind of ball, but of a lower quality? Is it clear from the case law whether this would be material?

## Hypo

Fred owns a small grocery store. He hired Wally to paint the inside of the store for $1,000. He could not be there when Wally started the job. When he came in on the second day of work, Wally and his workers had already painted half of the store.

In the contract between Fred and Wally, it said that Wally should use Colorama brand paint, a brand that had been recommended to Fred. However, Fred noticed that the workers were using Paintmaster brand paint instead. When Fred asked Wally why he was using Paintmaster, he replied that it was just as good as Colorama, cost the same, and was more easily available.

Fred was very angry that Wally ignored part of the contract, so he sent him and his workers home. They have not been allowed to come back and finish the work.

Assume for the purposes of this exercise that all experts agree that the quality of Paintmaster paint is just as high as that of Colorama.

**Question:** Fred would like to fire Wally and have someone else finish the job. Can he do this? (Remember to use one of the variations of the IRAC structure when writing your answer.)

## Exercise 2    False imprisonment[5]

Read the following law from the fictional jurisdiction of Collody and the exercises that follow. Then, read the hypo and answer the question given using any variation on the IRAC form.

### Lead-in

1.  The word "imprisonment" is usually associated with the state locking someone up in a secure building. Is that the only way that a person's freedom can be taken away?
2.  Compare the statute below to the kidnapping statutes in chapter 1. What similarities and differences do you notice? Which differences have to do with the fact that this a tort law statute, rather than a criminal one?

## Analysis of the statute

**Match the following words with the correct definition:**

| Word | Definition |
| --- | --- |
| 1. reasonable | a.  someone who buys and sells goods for profit |
| 2. tort | b.  sensible, logical, based on evidence |
| 3. merchant | c.  a wrongful act that harms someone |
| 4. prudent | d.  showing good judgement |

## Collody legal authorities

### Statutes

*Collody Civil Code section 232, False imprisonment:*
A person can be held liable for the tort of false imprisonment if he or she intentionally prevents a person from exiting a place, or makes it unsafe for him or her to exit.

*Collody Civil Code section 233, Merchant's privilege:*

a)  A merchant who has probable cause to believe that another is attempting to take goods from the merchant's property without paying may prevent that person from leaving for the time necessary for a reasonable investigation of the facts.

b)  Detaining a person in accordance with section (a) will not give rise to criminal or tort liability.

c)  Probable cause is defined as an honest belief in the guilt of the person to be detained, based on reasonable grounds. Reasonable grounds are facts and circumstances that would cause a normally prudent and cautious person to believe that a person has taken or is in the process of taking goods from the merchant's property without paying for them.

## Case summaries

### Rock's v. Disco, 4 Cdy. 09 (1973)

A security guard at Rock's Clothing saw Joe Disco take a men's wallet from a shelf and put it into his pocket. The guard grabbed him and took him into a back room where he was detained until police came. Disco sued for false imprisonment, claiming that the guard had no probable cause to detain him. Disco argued that he had merely put the wallet in his pocket to see if it felt comfortable, and that this was a normal action that should not have made anyone suspicious. At trial, Rock's was found liable for false imprisonment. The court of appeals affirmed. The court reasoned that simply putting an item in a place where store workers cannot see it is not, by itself, enough for probable cause. A normally prudent person would have realized that there was an innocent explanation for what Disco was doing. The security guard should have watched and waited for more evidence before detaining him.

### Mustard v. Mayo, 5 Cdy. 999 (1999)

Mustard was observed putting a magazine under his jacket in Mayo's bookshop. When Mayo saw Mustard start walking toward the door, he blocked Mustard's way and refused to let him leave. Mustard sued for false imprisonment, claiming that he had intended to pay for the item. The jury found for Mayo, and Mustard appealed. Mustard claimed that this case was just like Rock's because the only evidence against him was that he put something where the shopkeeper could not see it. The court of appeals affirmed. The court noted that this case was different than Rock's because (1) while a person buying a wallet might have an innocent reason for putting it in his pocket (seeing how it feels), that is not the case with putting a magazine under your jacket at a bookshop, and (2) the fact that Mustard had started walking toward the door was additional evidence of his intent to steal. Therefore, whether Mustard actually intended to pay for the magazine or not, Mayo had probable cause to detain him.

### Mark the following statements as True (T) or False (F):

1. A person can be liable for the tort of false imprisonment if they negligently prevent someone from leaving a building. **T / F**
2. A merchant will not be liable for false imprisonment if the merchant's privilege applies and the merchant satisfies the requirements of Civil Code section 233. **T / F**
3. If a merchant has probable cause to believe that a person is stealing something from their store, they can detain the suspect for as long as it takes to make them confess. **T / F**
4. The existence of probable cause requires both that (1) a merchant genuinely believes that a person is trying to take something from their store without paying, and that (2) a normally prudent and cautious person would agree. **T / F**

### Multiple choice—choose the best answer:

1. What is the best statement of the legal issue in *Rock's v. Disco*?
    a. Did the merchant's privilege apply to the security guard?
    b. When the security guard detained Disco, did he have a genuine belief that Disco was trying to steal the wallet?
    c. When Disco put the wallet in his back pocket, would a normally prudent and cautious person have believed that he had probable cause to detain him?
    d. Did the security guard falsely imprison Disco?
2. How does the court in *Mustard v. Mayo* distinguish *Rock's v. Disco*?
    a. A normally prudent person would have realized that there was an innocent explanation for Disco's behavior. However, there was no innocent explanation for Mustard's behavior.
    b. While Rock's was clearly liable for false imprisonment, Mayo was not.
    c. The security guard in Rock's took the customer into a back room to wait for the police. In contrast, Mayo merely made it unsafe for Mustard to exit.
    d. A normally cautious person would have realized that it was not safe to put a magazine under their jacket at a bookshop.

## Hypo

Barbara entered the Paymore supermarket in Collody City. She was just planning to buy some shampoo. She did not take a shopping basket when she entered because she was only going to buy one thing, and she had her own canvas shopping bag with her.

Barbara was confused by all of the different kinds of shampoo and wasn't sure which one was right for her kind of hair. She picked up a bottle of shampoo that she had a question about and put it in her bag. Before she could start walking toward the front counter to ask the cashier a question about it, the manager and a store security guard approached her and asked her to show them what was in the bag. The manager told Barbara that as soon as she put the shampoo in her bag, she was shoplifting.

Store security prevented her from leaving for 15 minutes while they waited for the police. Police officers questioned her for another 15 minutes before deciding not to arrest her.

Can Barbara successfully sue Paymore for false imprisonment under Collody law?

## Exercise 3    Burglary/Theft

Below is some law from the fictional jurisdiction of Collody relating to burglary and theft. Read the statutes and case summaries, and then answer the questions that follow.

After that, read the hypo and attempt to answer the question using any variation on the IRAC form. Before you start to write, you should spend some time spotting the issue, or issues, and planning your answer.

## Lead-in

1. Does the word "home" mean exactly the same thing as the word "house"?
2. Can a car or a boat be a home? If so, what may distinguish cars or boats that are homes from those that are not?

## Collody legal authorities

### Statutes[6]

*Collody Penal Code section 45. Burglary, defined:*
1. Anyone who breaks into and then enters someone else's home, at night, with the intent to commit a felony, is guilty of burglary.

2.  For purposes of this section:
    a.  "Breaking" means entering a home without permission, using the slightest amount of force (even pushing open a door).
    b.  "Home" means any place where a person lives.
    c.  The "entering" requirement is satisfied if any part of the body, even just a hand, enters the home.

*Collody Penal Code section 19. Theft:*
1.  Anyone who intentionally takes someone else's property without permission, with the intent to keep it, is guilty of theft.
    a.  If the property is worth more than $200, it is grand theft.
    b.  If the property is worth $200 or less, it is petty theft.

        . . .

2.  Grand theft is a felony.
3.  Petty theft is a misdemeanor.

## Case summaries

### People v. Jasper, 8 Cdy. 234 (2001)[7]

A woman got tired while driving and pulled over to the side of the road to sleep in her car. While she was sleeping, defendant broke the window and took her purse from the seat. The jury found the defendant guilty of theft and burglary. Defendant appealed the burglary conviction only, arguing that he had not stolen from a home. The court of appeal agreed. The court explained that "the victim lived in an apartment, not in her car. Sleeping somewhere for a few hours does not turn it into a home."

### People v. Slate, 8 Cdy. 257 (2003)

Defendant stole money from a tent where the victim lived. The victim had been living in the tent for 3 years. The jury found the defendant guilty of burglary for stealing money from the victim's home. The court of appeal agreed and affirmed the judgment. The court explained that "a tent can be a home for the purposes of Penal Code section 45. The victim had been living in the tent for three years and had no other place of residence. It clearly was her home."

### People v. Flint, 9 Cdy. 578 (2018)

Defendant was convicted of burglary after he broke into his neighbor's house and took the television from the living room. Defendant proved that he, and not his neighbor, was the rightful owner of the TV. The court of appeal reversed the conviction, explaining that "to be guilty of burglary a defendant must intend to commit a felony. Here, the defendant did not intend to commit theft, because he did not intend to take someone else's property. He intended to take his own property."

## Analysis of the statutes

**Find a word that means:**

1. a serious crime
2. a minor crime
3. a desire to do something

**Mark the following statements as True (T) or False (F):**

1. Breaking a window of a home is most likely sufficient to satisfy the definition of "breaking" in section 2 a. of the statute. **T / F**
2. The definition of "home" would most likely include a garden shed used by the owner to store gardening tools. **T / F**
3. According to Collody case law, you are not guilty of theft if you do not intend to take property that belonged to another person. **T / F**

**Think about the following questions:**

1. How have the courts clarified the meaning of "home" with regard to section 45 of the Collody Penal Code? What factors would likely be taken into account if a court had to consider in a subsequent case the question of whether something was a "home" for the purposes of this statute?
2. For a defendant to be found guilty of a section 19 theft offense, what three things must the prosecution prove?
3. In the *People v. Flint* case, what was the court's reason for overturning the defendant's conviction for burglary?

**Consider the facts in the hypo below. Then, answer the question given at the end using any variation on the IRAC form:**

David lost his job. With no money, he was forced to move out of his apartment on April 17, 2023. He had to live in his car. Although he usually slept in the car, he sometimes slept at his friend Antonio's house on the weekends, when he went there to take a shower and do his laundry.

His only valuable possession was a painting, which was worth $400. David kept it on the back seat of his car.

When David came back to his car on the night of May 23, 2023, he saw that one of his car's windows had been broken and that the painting was missing.

Police arrested a man named Robert after someone reported seeing him break the car's window at about 10:00 p.m. He had the painting in his hands when they caught him. When asked why he took the painting, Robert said that it actually belonged to him. According to Robert, it had been stolen from his house several months previously. Robert is telling the truth about this, and he genuinely believes that the painting is the one that was stolen from him, but he is mistaken.

Is Robert guilty of burglary?

**Note:** The following exercises use excerpts from real statutes and cases taken from various state jurisdictions of the United States. While based on real cases, the case reports have been edited for brevity for the purposes of this exercise.

## Exercise 4    Vandalism (United States)

We already covered the *Nicholas Y.* case in chapter 2. You may want to refer back to the exercises you did. Let's now see how that case and the relevant statute to which it refers applies to the following hypo. Answer the question given at the end of the hypo using any variation on the IRAC form.

Roland's mother became angry when 15-year-old Roland attempted to leave the house after he refused to attend school. A short confrontation occurred, with mother and son apparently pushing each other. Roland then went to the garage and got a baseball bat. He struck the kitchen table with the bat while his mother stood nearby. He hit it hard enough to cause paint from the bat to transfer to the table.

There was no other damage to the table.

Roland was charged with vandalism, among other crimes. Roland appealed his vandalism conviction.[8] Should the court reverse his conviction?

## California legal authorities

### Statute

*California Penal Code § 594*

(a) Every person who maliciously commits any of the following acts with respect to any real or personal property not his or her own . . . is guilty of vandalism:

    (1)  Defaces with graffiti or other inscribed material, [or]

    (2)  Damages [or]

    (3)  Destroys.

Case

85 Cal.App.4th 941, 102 Cal.Rptr.2d 511
Court of Appeal, Second District, Division 4, California.
In re NICHOLAS Y., a Person Coming Under the Juvenile Court Law.
The People, Plaintiff and Respondent,
v.
Nicholas Y., Defendant and Appellant.

Dec. 21, 2000.

. . .

<u>EPSTEIN</u>, Acting P.J.

Appellant Nicholas Y. appeals from [his conviction]. He contends the evidence was insufficient to prove he violated Penal Code section 594 (vandalism). . . . [W]e hold that writing on the glass window of a projection booth of a motion picture theater constituted defacing, and hence vandalism within the meaning of the statute. . . .

## I. FACTUAL SUMMARY

The evidence . . . proved that in the early morning hours of February 11, 2000, appellant wrote on a glass window of a projection booth at an A.M.C. theater with a Sharpie marker. After his arrest, appellant admitted to police that he had written "RTK" on the window. . . . Appellant said the initials stood for "The Right to Crime."

At the close of the prosecution's case, appellant's counsel argued that no defacing of or damage to property had been proved, stating: "[i]t's a piece of glass with a marker on it. You take a rag and wipe it off. End of case. It's ridiculous." The prosecutor countered that appellant trespassed and left fresh marks on the window, thus defacing the window with graffiti. The court found that appellant violated Penal Code section 594, subdivision (a), a misdemeanor.

## DISCUSSION
### I

Penal Code section 594 provides, in relevant part: "(a) Every person who maliciously commits any of the following acts with respect to any real or personal property not his or her own, in cases other than those specified by state law, is guilty of vandalism: (1) Defaces with graffiti or other inscribed material. . . . As used in this section the term 'graffiti or other inscribed material' includes any unauthorized inscription, word, figure, mark, or design that is written, marked, etched, scratched, drawn, or painted on real or personal property."

Appellant contends he did not violate the statute because the word "deface" [means] a "permanent alteration" of the surface of an object rather than the easily removed marking he placed on the window. He compares the facts of this case to chalk writing on a sidewalk held not to constitute vandalism in violation of Penal Code section 594 in *Mackinney v. Nielsen* 69 F.3d 1002 (9th Cir.1995). As appellant acknowledges, however, the statutory language interpreted in that case was different, making it "illegal to (1) *deface 'with paint or any other liquid,'* (2) damage or (3) destroy any real or personal property that is not one's own." (*Id.* at p. 1005, emphasis added.) The [court of appeal] reasoned that chalk is not a liquid and did not damage the sidewalk. Therefore, it found the defendant did not violate the statute. (*Ibid.*) The Legislature subsequently amended the statute to delete the phrase "defaces with paint or any other liquid" and substitute in its place the phrase "defaces with graffiti or other inscribed material." Accordingly, the *Mackinney* case is of no assistance to appellant's cause.

. . .

Graffiti may be, and regularly is, created with marker pens. (See *Sherwin-Williams Co. v. City of Los Angeles* (1993) 4 Cal.4th 893, 901, 16 Cal.Rptr.2d 215, 844 P.2d 534.) It would be irrational to hold that use of a marker pen on, for example, a painted or stucco surface constitutes vandalism in violation of Penal Code section 594, subdivision (a)(1) while use of a marker pen on glass is not. Each mars the surface with graffiti, which must be removed in order to restore the original condition. This pragmatic fact is consistent with the primary meaning of the word deface as defined in the Oxford English Dictionary: "To mar the face, features, or appearance of; to spoil or ruin the figure, form, or beauty of; to disfigure." . . . This definition does not incorporate an element of permanence. Thus, it appears that a marring of the surface is no less a defacement because it is more easily removed. It follows that appellant was properly found to have violated Penal Code section 594, subdivision (a)(1).

. . .

## DISPOSITION

For the foregoing reasons, the judgment is affirmed.

HASTINGS, and CURRY, JJ., concur.

## Exercise 5    Assault (United States)

### Lead-in

The following statute and cases relate to the crime of assault. First, read the short extract below and answer the questions.

Assault is a deliberate act causing someone to fear immediate harm or the application of force. In legal terms, assault does not necessarily involve physical contact; rather, it revolves around the apprehension of harm. It is crucial to distinguish assault from battery, where physical harm is inflicted. The key elements of assault in most jurisdictions include intent and reasonable apprehension. The offender must intentionally create a situation where the victim reasonably fears harm. For instance, pointing a weapon or making threats can constitute assault. Self-defense and consent are potential defenses against assault charges. Courts consider the context and the perceived threat when evaluating the reasonableness of apprehension.

**Mark the following statements as True (T) or False (F):**

1.  Assault always involves physical contact. **T / F**
2.  Assault requires the victim to reasonably fear harm. **T / F**
3.  Assault is a deliberate act. **T / F**
4.  Assault is defined as the application of force. **T / F**
5.  Courts do not consider the context when evaluating the reasonableness of apprehension. **T / F**

**Complete the sentences below using words from the box.**

| | | | |
|---|---|---|---|
| conditional | threaten | imminent | objective |
| | unambiguous | apprehension | |

1.  As the man walked toward John, he took out a knife. John felt great _______ and started to shake with fear.
2.  Jill's boss came within a few centimeters of her face and shouted at her loudly to finish the quote he had asked for, or else he would fire her. "Please don't try to _______ me," she replied, "I'm not scared of you!"
3.  The term of the contract was _______. There was only one way it could be interpreted.

4.  The judge came into the courtroom and everybody stood up. After months of preparation, the start of the trial was now ______.
5.  The test of intent under the statute was ______. In other words, it depended on what a reasonable person would believe in those circumstances, not on what the defendant said they were thinking.
6.  The offer made to the defendant was ______. If he confessed to the crime, his sentence would be reduced.

**Read the following hypo and the law from Texas that follows. There are then some questions that will help you prepare to write an answer to the hypo. After you have answered these questions, try to answer the question in the hypo using any variation on the IRAC form.**

Andrew Miller was playing baseball with his children when a group of teenagers started jeering and making offensive comments to the family. Andrew told his children to stay where they were and then approached the youths. As he walked over, one of the teenagers, who was very tall and well-built, and who appeared to be the leader of the group, called out 'OK, grandpa is coming over to start something'.

Andrew stopped two feet in front of the youth and replied, "If you talk like that to me and my family again, you will regret it." The youth laughed, saying, "Oh are we supposed to be scared? What you gonna do, grandpa?"

At that second, Andrew lost his temper and went back to where he had been playing baseball and picked up a bat. He walked back to the youth, swinging the bat in front of him and in the direction of the youth. Andrew shouted aggressively, "Just try me and you will see. I will knock your head off," and then swung the bat in the air a few times.

The teenagers ran off. Subsequently, the police arrived on the scene, having been directed to Andrew by members of the group of teenagers involved in the incident. He was arrested and charged with assault under Texas Penal Code s.22.01(a)(2).

Is Andrew guilty of assault? (For the purposes of the answer, cover only the charge of assault. You do not need to refer to possible defenses of provocation, etc.)

**Some questions to help you focus on the statute and cases:**

1.  Does Andrew make any physical contact with the youths? Do you need to cause bodily injury to be found guilty of assault under the statute? Why or why not?
2.  Having read the *Tidwell v. State of Texas* case, does it make a difference that Andrew made a *conditional* threat to the youths (that is, if they

continued, he would act, etc.)? Are there other factors in the *Tidwell* case that the court would consider in respect of Andrew?

3. Andrew wants to rely on the *Jones v. Shipley* case in his defense. In what ways could this case be distinguished from *Tidwell?*
4. Did the court in the *Moore v. City of Wylie* case make any clarifications of the law on assault? Do you think it is relevant to the hypo?

## Texas legal authorities

### Statute

*V.T.C.A., Penal Code § 22.01. Assault*

(a) A person commits an offense if the person:
   (1) intentionally, knowingly, or recklessly causes bodily injury to another, including the person's spouse;
   (2) intentionally or knowingly threatens another with imminent bodily injury, including the person's spouse; or
   (3) intentionally or knowingly causes physical contact with another when the person knows or should reasonably believe that the other will regard the contact as offensive or provocative.

### Cases

187 S.W.3d 771

Court of Appeals of Texas,

Texarkana.

Elizabeth Ann TIDWELL, Appellant,

v.

The STATE of Texas, Appellee.

No. 06–05–00113–CR.

|

Submitted Feb. 23, 2006.

|

Decided March 1, 2006.

**Synopsis**

**Background:** Defendant was convicted in the 5th Judicial District Court, Cass County, Ralph Burgess, J., of aggravated assault by threat. Defendant appealed.

**Holdings:** The Court of Appeals, Carter, J., held that:
evidence was legally sufficient to support finding that defendant's threat to victim caused a reasonable apprehension by victim of imminent bodily injury, as required to support conviction. . . .

Affirmed.

Attorneys and Law Firms

Craig L. Henry, Texarkana, for appellant.
Tina Richardson, Asst. Dist. Atty., Linden, for appellee.
Before MORRISS, C.J., ROSS and CARTER, JJ.

## OPINION

Opinion by Justice CARTER.

Elizabeth Ann Tidwell was found guilty by the trial court of aggravated assault by threatening John Spann, a Cass County deputy, with imminent bodily injury and using or exhibiting a deadly weapon, a firearm. The trial court assessed her punishment at five years' confinement. On appeal, she alleges the evidence was legally insufficient to sustain the conviction. Having found the evidence legally sufficient, we affirm the trial court's judgment.

## I. Factual Background

For a number of years, the Texas Child Protective Services (CPS) has interacted with Tidwell concerning the welfare of Tidwell's children. On July 30, 2003, the CPS contacted the Cass County Sheriff's Department for assistance in investigating Tidwell concerning the care of her children. Dale Gentry, a deputy for the sheriff's office, accompanied the CPS staff person to Tidwell's residence and found her outside with her two children. Tidwell returned inside the home, and Gentry followed onto the porch. As Gentry was attempting to talk with Tidwell, she said she was not giving up her children and that she had a gun and would shoot him. Gentry reported that he needed assistance, and Spann, who was nearby, arrived a few minutes later. Spann was driving a marked police vehicle and was wearing his uniform. Spann positioned himself to watch the back door of the house. Within five or ten minutes, Tidwell came out the back door of the house with two children and was holding a black revolver in her hand. Spann told her to drop the gun, and she replied, " 'You better get away from me or—' . . . 'Get the f—— away from me' . . . 'or I'll shoot you.' " Spann then backed away, and Tidwell took the children back into the house. Sometime later, Lieutenant Ray Copeland arrived on the scene and negotiated with Tidwell. Ultimately, Tidwell allowed the officers to enter and search the home. Tidwell led the officers to a .22 pistol located in a closet. No shells were found inside the pistol, and no ammunition for it was found in the house. Tidwell was arrested and gave a statement the following day that she thought the gun she had in her hand was a BB gun [an air gun that shoots pellets].

Tidwell asserts that the evidence is legally insufficient to prove she committed the offense. . . .

. . .

## A. Assault

Tidwell maintains that the language attributed to her, which in essence was, "Get away or I will shoot you," is not adequate to present a threat of imminent bodily injury. . . .

. . .

Our law of assault by threat requires proof that one acts with intent to cause a reasonable apprehension of imminent bodily injury. *Garrett v. State*, 619 S.W.2d 172, 173 (Tex.Crim.App. [Panel Op.] 1981); *Torres v. State*, 905 S.W.2d 440 (Tex.App.-Fort Worth 1995, no pet.). . . . [F]or our decision today, the court must examine whether Tidwell's statements and actions constituted a threat that bodily injury was imminent. . . .

. . . [A] threat of harm on the occurrence or nonoccurrence of a future event does not necessarily mean that the harmful consequences threatened are not imminent. The focus of the inquiry should be whether the threat was "imminent"—not merely whether the threat was conditional. *See Neagle v. State*, 91 S.W.3d 832, 834 (Tex.App.-Fort Worth 2002, pet. ref'd) (citing *In re A.C.*, 48 S.W.3d 899, 904 (Tex.App.-Fort Worth 2001, pet. denied)). For instance, it would be nonsensical to conclude that, if a person, while using and exhibiting a deadly weapon, said, "Don't move or I will shoot," or, "Give me the money or I will shoot," such statements are merely conditional and could not convey a threat of imminent bodily injury. . . . On the other hand, threatening to kill a police officer while the defendant was handcuffed would only constitute a threat of future harm which might occur after the defendant was released from jail, and did not present an "imminent" threat. *See Hill v. State*, 844 S.W.2d 937 (Tex.App.-Eastland 1992, no pet.). . . .

The gist of the offense of assault, as set out in Section 22.01(a)(2), is that one acts with intent to cause a reasonable apprehension of imminent bodily injury (though not necessarily with intent to inflict such harm). *Garrett*, 619 S.W.2d at 174. Here, Tidwell had in her possession a black revolver and stated to Spann that, unless he left, she would shoot him. Spann was lawfully and properly on the property for official duties associated with the Cass County Sheriff's Department. Even though Tidwell did not point the gun toward Spann, he testified the threat placed him in fear of bodily harm and he backed away for his own safety. We find that Tidwell's threat caused a reasonable apprehension by Spann of imminent bodily injury. Threats may be communicated verbally as well as communicated by conduct. *McGowan v. State,* 664 S.W.2d 355, 357 (Tex.Crim.App.1984); *Nemecek v. State,* 621 S.W.2d 404 (Tex.Crim.App. [Panel Op.] 1980). Here, the threat was by a combination of words ("Get the f—— away from me . . . or I'll shoot you") as well as by conduct (the use of a deadly weapon). The mere presence of a deadly weapon, under proper circumstances, can be enough to instill fear and threaten a person with bodily injury. We find the evidence to be legally sufficient to allow a rational trier of fact to find Tidwell guilty of the assault beyond a reasonable doubt.

. . .

We affirm the judgment of the trial court.

508 S.W.3d 766
Court of Appeals of Texas, Houston (1st Dist.).
Vicsandra JONES and Darren Jones, Individually and as Next Friends of
John Doe, a Minor, Appellants
v.
Josi Calderon SHIPLEY, Appellee
NO. 01–16–00046–CV

|

Opinion issued December 8, 2016

|

Rehearing En Banc Overruled January 31, 2017

**Synopsis**

**Background:** Second-grade student's parents brought action against chaperone of school field trip for assault by threat of bodily injury, alleging that chaperone rushed toward student and shook her finger at him while stating she would "get him." The 61st District Court, Harris County, dismissed action. Parents appealed.

The Court of Appeals, Rebeca Huddle, J., held that alleged words and conduct of school chaperone did not constitute an objective threat of imminent bodily injury, as required to state a claim for assault.

Affirmed.

Laura Carter Higley, J., dissented and filed opinion.

**Procedural Posture(s):** On Appeal; Motion to Dismiss.

On Appeal from the 61st District Court, Harris County, Texas, Trial Court Case No. 2015–56901

## Attorneys and Law Firms

Michael C. Watson, Houston, TX, for Appellants.

Tanya N. Garrison, Weycer, Kaplan, Pulaski & Zuber, PC, Houston, TX, for Appellee.

Panel consists of Chief Justice Radack and Justices Higley and Huddle.

## OPINION

Rebeca Huddle, Justice

While chaperoning a school field trip, Josi Calderon Shipley allegedly rushed toward a second grader, John Doe, and shook her finger at him while stating she would "get him." John Doe's parents, Vicsandra Jones and Darren Jones, sued Shipley for assault by threat of bodily injury. The trial court granted Shipley's motion to dismiss under Texas Rule of Civil Procedure 91a. On appeal, the Joneses argue that the trial court erred by granting the motion. We affirm.

## Background

The Joneses alleged in their First Amended Original Petition that they had an unpleasant exchange with Shipley shortly after they enrolled John Doe in the second grade of a new school. According to the amended petition, Shipley, the mother of another student at the same school, told Vicsandra and John Doe that John Doe was a "monster" and "completely out of control at school." The Joneses also alleged that Shipley said "she was going to see to it that he was expelled" from the school, adding that she and other parents at the school "pay high tuition rates to keep their children away from kids like [John Doe]."

The incident that forms the basis of the Joneses' suit for assault by threat of bodily injury took place about a week later, according to the amended petition. The Joneses allege that Shipley was chaperoning John Doe's school field trip to the zoo when she saw John Doe sitting alone, "rushed over" to him from 50 feet away in "an extremely threatening and aggressive manner," "put her finger inches from his face," and "told him she was going to 'get him.'" The amended petition alleges that this "attack" was without provocation, and caused John Doe to have a "fear of imminent bodily injury" and "severe emotional trauma."

Shipley filed a Rule 91a motion to dismiss, arguing that assuming all of the facts pleaded by the Joneses to be true, they were insufficient to support a cause of action for assault by threat of bodily injury. The Joneses responded, arguing that they had pleaded sufficient facts to state a claim for assault by threat of bodily injury. The trial court granted the motion, dismissing the case and awarding Shipley attorney's fees under Rule 91a.

### Discussion

In their sole issue, the Joneses argue that the trial court erred by granting Shipley's Rule 91a motion to dismiss.

. . .

## B. Applicable Law

The elements of assault are the same in both criminal and civil cases. *See Loaisiga v. Cerda*, 379 S.W.3d 248, 256 (Tex. 2012). A person commits assault if the person:

(1)  intentionally, knowingly, or recklessly causes bodily injury to another, including the person's spouse;
(2)  intentionally or knowingly threatens another with imminent bodily injury, including the person's spouse; or
(3)  intentionally or knowingly causes physical contact with another when the person knows or should reasonably believe that the other will regard the contact as offensive or provocative.

Tex. Penal Code § 22.01(a). The focus in an assault by threat case is on the defendant's words and conduct, and the critical inquiry is whether a reasonable person under the circumstances would consider the words and conduct to be an objective threat of imminent bodily injury. *See Olivas v. State*, 203 S.W.3d 341, 347 (Tex. Crim. App. 2006) ("Although the question whether the defendant's conduct produced fear in the victim is relevant, the crucial inquiry remains whether the assailant acted in such a manner as would under the circumstances portend an immediate threat of danger to a person of reasonable sensibility.") . . . .

## C. Analysis

The Joneses, who sued individually and as next friends of John Doe, do not allege that Shipley caused John Doe bodily injury, nor do they allege Shipley caused any physical contact with him. Rather, the Joneses allege assault of the variety described in Section 22.01(a)(2): threatening another with imminent bodily injury. Texas authorities demonstrate that Shipley's alleged words and conduct cannot amount to assault by threatening imminent bodily injury as a matter of law. The cases in which conduct has been held sufficient to constitute assault by threat of imminent bodily injury involve words and conduct that, viewed from the objective perspective of a reasonable person, constitute express and unambiguous threats of imminent bodily injury, frequently death. . . .

While liability for assault can be based on a threat of imminent bodily injury short of death, the authorities in which evidence has been found sufficient to establish an assault under 22.01(a)(2) involve words and conduct, that, unlike Shipley's vague alleged threat to "get" John Doe, constitute unambiguous threats of imminent bodily injury from the objective perspective of a reasonable person. . . . [I]n *Tidwell v. State*, 186 S.W.3d 773 (Tex. App.–Texarkana 2006, pet. stricken), the court of appeals held that legally sufficient evidence supported the defendant's assault conviction where the defendant had a gun in her possession and told the complainant that, unless he left, she would shoot him. *Id.* at 775. . . .

By contrast, conduct and words objectively more threatening than Shipley's words and conduct in this case have been held *not* to constitute assault by threat of imminent bodily injury. For example, *Texas Bus Lines v. Anderson*, 233 S.W.2d 961, 963 (Tex. Civ. App.–Galveston 1950, writ ref'd n.r.e.), involved an altercation between a bus driver and his would-be passenger. When a ticket agent instructed the bus driver to refuse Anderson entry to the bus, Anderson nevertheless sought to board, and the driver, who was standing inside the bus near the door, "angrily" said to Anderson and his companion, who were standing outside the bus's door, "You can't ride on my bus under any circumstances—Neither of you sons of b****** can ride my bus under any circumstances." *Id.* at 963. As he said this, the bus driver was positioned on the stairs inside the bus, "braced" and "ready to kick [Anderson] in the face" if he tried to force his way onto the bus. *Id.* Yet the appellate court held this did not raise a fact issue on assault by threat and it was error for the trial judge to have submitted the claim. *Id.* at 964; *see also Moore v. City of Wylie*, 319 S.W.3d 778, 782–83 (Tex. App.–El Paso 2010, no pet.) (even though plaintiff was "terrified during the confrontation," no fact issue on assault by threat of imminent bodily injury where supervisor, while reprimanding plaintiff, poked him in the chest with his finger three or four times).

Shipley's alleged words and conduct are a far cry from the type of conduct that has been held to constitute assault by threat of imminent bodily injury. The act of walking "aggressively" toward John Doe and shaking her finger at him, together with the vague verbal threat to "get" him, does not support a reasonable inference in the mind of a reasonable person that Shipley made an objective threat to inflict imminent bodily injury on the second grader during a school-sponsored field trip to the zoo. This is particularly true given the Joneses' allegation that what Shipley had threatened a week earlier, when she spoke more precisely, was expulsion from the school, which is neither bodily injury nor imminent. Assuming the truth of the Joneses' allegations, Shipley's vague threat to "get" John Doe together with her aggressive walking and finger-shaking during a school field trip do not constitute an objective threat of imminent bodily injury to a person of reasonable sensibility in light of the circumstances. Because the words and conduct alleged, though unkind, are insufficient to hold Shipley liable for assault by threat, we hold that the trial court correctly dismissed the Joneses' suit under Rule 91a.

### Conclusion

We affirm the trial court's judgment.

. . .

319 S.W.3d 778
Court of Appeals of Texas,
El Paso.
James Randall MOORE a/k/a Randy Moore, Appellant,
v.
CITY OF WYLIE, Texas and William Johnson, Appellees.
No. 08–08–00039–CV.

|

Feb. 17, 2010.

## Synopsis

**Background:** Former city employee filed suit against the city and supervisor for assault. The 416th District Court, Collin County, Chris Oldner, J., entered summary judgment for city and supervisor, and employee appealed.
**Holdings:** The Court of Appeals, Ann Crawford McClure, J., held that: employee, who alleged that supervisor poked employee in and around the chest area, did not establish claim for civil assault.

. . .

Affirmed.
**Procedural Posture(s):** On Appeal; Motion for Summary Judgment.

Attorneys and Law Firms

Michael Patrick Kelly, Law Office of Michael P. Kelly, Dallas, for Appellant.

William W. Krueger III, Martin, Disiere, Jefferson & Wisdom, LLP, Dallas, for Appellee.

Before CHEW, C.J., McCLURE, and RIVERA, JJ.

## OPINION

ANN CRAWFORD McCLURE, Justice.

James Randall Moore, a/k/a Randy Moore, appeals from a summary judgment granted in favor of the City of Wylie, Texas and William Johnson. Finding no error, we affirm.

## FACTUAL SUMMARY

The City of Wylie hired Randy Moore as a building inspector on March 15, 2004. William Johnson, a senior building inspector, served as Moore's supervisor. On December 16, 2004, Johnson called Moore into his office and reprimanded him for attendance problems. When Moore questioned him, Johnson allegedly poked Moore in the chest with his finger three or four times and told him to do his job. Moore did not report the incident immediately, but he did tell another building inspector, Keith Moore, about the confrontation. He also sought medical attention later in the day when he began suffering from tightness in the chest. The emergency room physician told Moore his symptoms were stress-related.

Moore . . . sued Johnson for assault . . . . Appellees filed a motion for traditional and no-evidence summary judgment with respect to the claim. Moore filed an initial response and two supplemental responses. The trial court granted the no-evidence summary judgment and Moore brings six issues for review [only the assault issue is covered below].

## CIVIL ASSAULT

. . . Moore challenges the summary judgment granted in Johnson's favor on the assault claim. The elements of civil assault mirror those required for criminal assault. *Umana v. Kroger Texas, L.P.*, 239 S.W.3d 434, 436 (Tex. App.-Dallas 2007, no pet.); *Johnson v. Davis*, 178 S.W.3d 230, 240 (Tex. App.-Houston [14th Dist.] 2005, pet. denied). Moore alleged in his first amended petition that Johnson "poked the Plaintiff in and around the chest area." He also asserted that Johnson intentionally, knowingly, or recklessly made contact with Moore which caused bodily injury and intentionally and knowingly threatened him with imminent bodily injury. A person commits assault if he:

(1) intentionally, knowingly, or recklessly causes bodily injury to another, including the person's spouse;
(2) intentionally or knowingly threatens another with imminent bodily injury, including the person's spouse; or
(3) intentionally or knowingly causes physical contact with another when the person knows or should reasonably believe that the other will regard the contact as offensive or provocative.

. . .

Under Section 22.01(a)(1), Moore was required to prove that he suffered bodily injury. The Penal Code defines bodily injury as "physical pain, illness, or any impairment of physical condition." Tex.Penal Code Ann. § 1.07(a)(8). Moore did not testify or offer any evidence that being poked in the chest caused bodily injury. Under Section 22.01(a)(2), Moore was required to prove that Johnson intentionally or knowingly threatened him with imminent bodily injury. Moore's testimony does not raise a fact issue on these elements. Because the trial court did not err by granting summary judgment on the assault cause of action, we overrule Issue One [the assault issue].

. . .

. . . For all of these reasons, we affirm the summary judgment.

## Exercise 6    Tort: Negligent supervision (United States)

### Lead-in

1. The law for the following exercise comes entirely from cases rather than a statute—which is quite common in tort law. In what ways, if any, will this fact require you to change the way that you approach this exercise?
2. What kind of liability should parents have for the harm that their minor children cause to others?
3. What situations can you think of where a person could take on the legal responsibility for someone else's child?

**Match the following words or phrases with the correct definition:**

| Word or phrase | Definition |
| --- | --- |
| 1. remand | a. predictable |
| 2. dispositive | b. a cause that creates legal liability |

| Word or phrase | Definition |
| --- | --- |
| 3. proximate cause | c. creates |
| 4. gives rise to | d. a decision by a judge in a jury trial that the defense wins because the plaintiff did not prove its case |
| 5. directed verdict | e. decisive or final |
| 6. foreseeable | f. to send a case back to a lower court for further action |

**Use each of the words or phrases above to fill in the blanks in the sentences below:**

1. The court granted a ______ because the plaintiff presented no evidence on one of the elements of the statute.
2. In order to prove negligence, the plaintiff must demonstrate that the defendant's actions were the ______ of their injuries.
3. The judge decided to ______ the case to a lower court for further proceedings.
4. The contract ______ rights and duties for both parties.
5. The lawyer's argument was so compelling that the court made a ______ ruling in her client's favor.
6. In this case, it was ______ that the defendant's failure to mop up the spilled juice would cause someone to slip and fall.

**The hypos below both involve the tort of "negligent supervision." Read them, as well as the three cases that follow. Then, answer the question given at the end of both the hypos using any variation on the IRAC form.**

Hypo 1[9]

Sam and Maryann Johnson agreed to let their 17-year-old daughter Sarah throw a party for her high school volleyball team on the farm where they lived. Among those Sarah invited was Amanda Baker. The Johnsons kept a three-wheel all-terrain vehicle (ATV) on their property.

That evening, another invited guest, Laura Fellows, began driving the ATV. Laura had never driven an ATV before. After she drove the ATV around the pasture a few times, Amanda climbed aboard as a passenger and the two of them drove toward the Johnsons' house.

On a path to the house, Laura and Amanda encountered Sarah, who was driving a tractor. To avoid hitting Sarah, Laura turned the vehicle but headed toward a creek. As the two approached the creek, Laura applied the brakes, but she could not stop in time, and the ATV went over the embankment and dropped six or seven feet into the dry creek bed. Amanda sustained numerous injuries.

Maryann arrived home after the accident, about three hours after the party started. Sam was never present as he was out of town. No other adults were present at the time of the accident, either.

Amanda and her family are suing Sam and Maryann Johnson for negligent supervision. Are they liable for this tort?

**Some questions to help you focus on some key elements of the cases:**

1.   Under Missouri law, what does the court in *Bequette v. Buff* say about any duty to supervise in relation to a claim for "negligent supervision"?
2.   On what grounds did the court in the *Bequette v. Buff* case rule against the plaintiff's claim? How might the facts of hypo 1 be distinguished from *Bequette v. Buff*?
3.   Are there any similarities in the facts of hypo 1 and the case of *Rogger v. Voyles*? How foreseeable is it that a young person may lose control of an ATV if they had never used one before?

Hypo 2[10]

Twelve-year-old Arlo and his family went to the Tortland amusement park for his birthday. Arlo decided to ride the Big Whirly ride—a ride that spins around at fairly high speeds. The riders are held in their seats by seatbelts. Arlo's parents did not want to ride with him, so they found a place to sit where they could see the ride from.

Before getting on the ride, an announcement instructed everyone to fasten their seatbelts. Arlo got into his seat and attempted to fasten his seatbelt.

Pete was the Tortland worker who was operating the ride. Before the ride started, he was supposed to make sure that everyone was wearing a seatbelt. Pete did this by walking around and glancing briefly at everyone's lap, the way that cabin crew do in an airplane before takeoff. Arlo did not tell Pete that he was having any trouble with his belt, and Pete did not notice a problem with the way that it was fastened.

Soon after Pete started the ride, Arlo was thrown out of his seat and was injured when he struck a fence.

Arlo later told his parents that the belt was "kind of stuck" because the buckle was "hard to push down." As a result, he felt that it was "sort of loose."

An independent investigation found no evidence of a mechanical failure that could have caused the accident. However, the investigators did find that some of the seatbelts required more pressure than others to close properly.

If Arlo and his family sue Pete for negligent supervision, will they win? What will happen if they sue Tortland as well?

**Some questions to help you focus on some key elements of the cases:**

1.  What is the relationship between Arlo and Pete in the hypo? How might the case of *Bequette v. Buff* be used in this regard?
2.  How do you think *Rogger v. Voyles* could be relevant to the facts in the hypo? Could Arlo's age be a factor that the court would take into account?
3.  In *Daugherty v. Allee's Sports Bar & Grill*, what did the court state as being the law with regard to an employer's liability for the tort of an employee?
4.  Do you think Pete was acting within the scope of his employment when he glanced at people's seatbelts on the ride?


## Missouri legal authorities

Cases

862 S.W.2d 921

Dustin BEQUETTE, Respondent,

v.

Patricia BUFF, Appellant.

No. 61896.

Missouri Court of Appeals,

Eastern District,

Division Four.

Sept. 7, 1993.

CRAHAN, Judge.

Patricia Buff ("Defendant") appeals from an adverse judgment of $25,000 entered pursuant to a jury verdict in a suit seeking to recover for personal injuries sustained by Dustin Bequette ("Plaintiff") in an altercation following a party at Defendant's home. On appeal, Defendant asserts that the trial court erred in refusing her motion for a directed verdict and alleges error in the instructions and in certain evidentiary rulings. We find Defendant's first point to be dispositive and reverse the judgment.

. . .

The record establishes that Defendant planned a party at her home in St. Louis for her son, John, to celebrate his sixteenth birthday. . . . Defendant told John that there could be no more than twenty people at the party, including him and his girlfriend. John gave Defendant a list of names of persons he intended to invite to the party, which did not include Plaintiff. . . .

In preparation for the party, Defendant purchased soda, chips and a sheet cake. She did not purchase any beer for the party or authorize anyone else to do so. . . .

. . .

On the day before the party, Plaintiff, a seventeen year old senior at DuBourg High School, was standing by his locker when a younger student, whom he did not know, came down the hall handing out flyers advertising a "Keg Party—All-U-Can-Drink $3.00" at Defendant's address on the following day. Plaintiff had never been to Defendant's home and was not a friend or schoolmate of John's, but had played soccer against him and knew him by sight. John attended a different school and was not the person who handed out the flyers. [The flyers were not prepared by Defendant or her son.]

. . .

As Plaintiff [and his friends] approached Defendant's front porch, there were two men situated outside the front door collecting money. One of the men [who was not identified at trial] had long blond hair and no shirt . . . .

. . .

Five or ten minutes after Plaintiff entered the house, the police arrived, broke up the party and ordered everyone to leave. As Plaintiff and his friends were leaving, the shirtless man who had collected their money told them to come back later to get their money back or drink. . . .

About a half hour to an hour later, Plaintiff and his friends returned to Defendant's house to get their money back. The door was closed and there were fewer cars parked on the street. Plaintiff, Jeff, and Joe went to the front door and knocked. The shirtless man answered and Plaintiff told him that he and his friends wanted their money back. The shirtless man told them to wait and shut the door. Shortly thereafter, the door opened and there were five or six individuals standing at the door, who told Plaintiff and his companions they were not going to get their money back. An argument ensued and someone Plaintiff did not know thrust a BB handgun toward Plaintiff. [2] Plaintiff reached to grab the gun and, in the scuffle, Plaintiff was pushed down the steps.

As a result of the fall, Plaintiff broke his right ankle. . . .

. . .

Plaintiff filed a petition stating separate counts against Defendant and Defendant's insurance carrier. The latter count was severed for separate trial.

In the first count, Plaintiff alleged that Defendant was negligent in various respects and the case was ultimately submitted to the jury on a theory of "negligent supervision." . . .

. . .

Defendant maintains that the trial court erred in denying her motion for a directed verdict because the evidence failed to establish any relationship between Defendant and Plaintiff which would give rise to any duty to protect him from the injury suffered. In fact, Defendant points out that she had no reason to know of Plaintiff's existence, let alone his presence on her property or his exposure to potential injury. In this regard, Defendant emphasizes the undisputed evidence that: 1) Defendant planned the party in advance with her son; 2) Defendant limited the number of guests to twenty and Plaintiff was not among the twenty invited guests; 3) Defendant did not issue the flyer or know about it prior to the date of the party; 4) Defendant provided soda, chips and cake; and 5) Defendant did not authorize or know about the serving of alcohol at the party. Under such circumstances, Defendant urges that the evidence was insufficient to establish any duty on her part to protect Plaintiff from injury or, for that matter, that any breach of duty occurred. We agree.

At trial and on appeal, Plaintiff somewhat confusingly attempts to justify submission on the ground that Missouri has recognized a tort of "negligent supervision" and that the evidence in this case establishes that Plaintiff failed to properly supervise the party. However, Plaintiff overlooks the fact that, to the extent Missouri cases recognize a cause of action for "negligent supervision," the duty to supervise runs not to an activity, but rather to an individual. The cases relied upon by Plaintiff to support his theory of negligent supervision uniformly involve situations where the plaintiff and the defendant have some relationship. . . .

Here, Plaintiff and Defendant did not have a relationship. The evidence was undisputed that Defendant and Plaintiff did not know each other; Plaintiff was not a friend of Defendant's son; Defendant had not invited Plaintiff to her home; Plaintiff was not among the twenty invited guests; and Defendant did not issue a general invitation or know of such an invitation prior to the party. We decline to extend the duty to supervise where there is no relationship.

. . .

For the foregoing reasons, the trial court's judgment on Count I of the petition is reversed and the cause is remanded with directions to enter judgment on Count I in favor of Defendant and for further proceedings consistent with this opinion.

CARL R. GAERTNER and CRANE, JJ., concur.

797 S.W.2d 844
Robert L. ROGGER, Sondra Rogger, and Tosha Rogger,
Plaintiffs-Respondents,
v.
Leonard A. VOYLES and Jane Lowe, Defendants-Appellants.
No. 16637.
Missouri Court of Appeals,
Southern District,
Division One.
Sept. 27, 1990.

PREWITT, Judge.

Plaintiffs sought damages as a result of personal injuries to plaintiff Tosha Rogger. Following nonjury trial, judgment was entered in favor of plaintiff Tosha Rogger and against defendants for $373,219 and in favor of [her parents] plaintiffs Robert L. Rogger and Sandra Rogger and against defendants for $16,478. Defendants appeal.

. . .

. . . Defendants contend plaintiffs "neither pleaded nor proved an actionable case of negligent supervision of an underaged driver by entrusting her with a motor vehicle in that they made no allegations nor offered any evidence that the underage driver's incompetency in the operation of the motor vehicle was the proximate cause of her harm or that appellants knew or should have known of brake problems so as to make her injuries foreseeable under the circumstances."

. . .

The principal facts are not in dispute. On September 30, 1981, Tosha Rogger, age 13, was visiting her maternal grandfather, defendant Leonard A. Voyles, on his farm in Camden County. Jane Lowe resided there with him. On that date, with both defendants' permission and knowledge, Tosha had been driving alone, off and on for approximately six-and-one-half hours, a 1971 Jeepster motor vehicle. She noticed that its brakes had not been operating properly. While operating the vehicle alone on a gravel road which went through the farm, she lost control of it, and it struck a ravine. She suffered serious personal injuries when her face hit the steering wheel. She testified that she lost control because the brakes did not work. Previous to that date, she had not driven a full-sized motor vehicle. She had driven a "go kart" on the farm when she was six or seven.

Plaintiffs' petition alleged defendants were negligent in several respects in allowing Tosha Rogger to drive while under their supervision, including that she had no previous driving experience, and that they failed to give her sufficient directions on how to properly and safely operate it. The petition stated that as a direct and proximate result of that negligence she was injured. As plaintiffs contend, it is a reasonable inference from the matters alleged that Tosha's lack of driving experience and direction was the proximate cause of her injuries. *Cf. Golden v. National Utilities Co.*, 356 Mo. 84, 201 S.W.2d 292, 298 (1947).

Three elements must exist for a case of actionable negligence: (1) a duty owed by defendant to protect plaintiff from the injury complained, (2) a failure to perform that duty, and (3) injury proximately caused by that failure. *Lavo v. Medlin*, 705 S.W.2d 562, 564 (Mo.App.1986). "The concept of duty depends upon the issue of reasonable foreseeability." *Id.*

Defendants had a duty to exercise reasonable or ordinary care in the supervision of Tosha. *Swain v. Simon*, 699 S.W.2d 769, 773 (Mo.App.1985). Ordinary care may require more vigilance and caution when a child is involved if there is a potentially dangerous situation of which a supervisor is or should be aware. *Id.*

[The court agrees with *Swain's* discussion of the duty of care. However, it does not fully agree with its explanation of what it means to breach that duty, which is important because defendants rely on it. According to *Swain*, something is foreseeable if] "a reasonable person could have foreseen that the injuries of the type suffered would likely occur under the circumstances. . . ."

We do not agree that foreseeability requires that an incident of this type "would likely occur", it is enough that a reasonable person would recognize that it could or might occur and that steps should be taken to prevent it. "[F]oreseeability is not to be measured by what is more probable than not, but includes whatever is likely enough in the setting of modern life that a reasonably thoughtful person would take account of it in guiding practical conduct." 3 Harper, James and Gray, The Law of Torts, § 18.2 at 657-659 (2d ed. 1986).

. . .

It is foreseeable that a minor who has never operated a full-size motor vehicle, but does so without direction or supervision, might lose control of it and suffer serious injuries. It is certainly possible, if not even "likely".

It is also more probable that an inexperienced operator such as Tosha might have that happen to her than to a more experienced operator. Although an experienced driver might lose control of a vehicle, it is far more likely to happen to one inexperienced and untutored in the operation of a motor vehicle.

That problems with the brakes may have caused or contributed to the collision, does not mean that defendants were not negligent. The trial court found that defendants were experienced with the vehicle Tosha was driving and the terrain of the farm and that defendants did not "exercise reasonable or ordinary care in taking care of Tosha". Although no specific finding was made as to how they were negligent, the trial court would have been justified in finding that defendants did not, as alleged in the petition, give Tosha sufficient direction on how to properly operate the vehicle or warn her of the dangers of the loose gravel roadway or were negligent in allowing her to operate the vehicle alone.

Under the circumstances, these would have been prudent things to do. Had defendants limited the area in which Tosha was driving to level terrain or prevented her from going on a roadway, then the collision might not have occurred. Had one or more of them been in the vehicle with her they might have so confined her or kept her at a speed where the brakes might not have been necessary to prevent the collision. There was sufficient evidence for the trier of fact to find that there was negligent supervision of Tosha, that her injuries were foreseeable, and that her incompetency in operating the motor vehicle was the cause of the collision and her resulting injuries. . . .

. . .

The judgment is affirmed.
MAUS, P.J., and CROW, J., concur.


260 S.W.3d 869

Missouri Court of Appeals, Western District.
Christopher A. DAUGHERTY, Appellant,
v.
ALLEE'S SPORTS BAR & GRILL, Respondent.
No. WD 68635

|

Aug. 26, 2008.

Opinion

THOMAS H. NEWTON, Judge.

Christopher A. Daugherty was an employee of the defendant, Allee's Sports Bar and Grill (Allee's). He was drinking off-duty at Allee's one night, while sitting with the General Manager of Allee's, Eric Walker, who was also off-duty. Off-duty employees are treated as customers at Allee's and receive no discounts for food and drink. Jamie Yoder was the bartender at Allee's that evening. Mr. Daugherty and Mr. Walker both ordered beer. Before serving beer to Mr. Daugherty, Ms. Yoder placed a toothpick in the beer. Ms. Yoder intended this action to be a practical joke. Mr. Daugherty, unaware of the toothpick, drank the beer. He swallowed the toothpick and was injured as a result. Mr. Walker testified that he was aware that "some joking around or horsing around took place" at Allee's.

Mr. Daugherty filed a petition for damages against Allee's. His petition alleged that Allee's was vicariously liable under the doctrine of respondeat superior for Ms. Yoder's acts . . . . Allee's filed a motion for summary judgment . . . . The trial court granted Allee's motion for summary judgment without explanation. Mr. Daugherty appeals.

. . .

## Legal Analysis

In his first point, Mr. Daugherty argues that the trial court erred in granting summary judgment because a genuine dispute existed as to whether Ms. Yoder was operating within the scope of her employment when she placed the toothpick in his beer. Allee's argued in its motion for summary judgment that it was entitled to judgment as a matter of law because the undisputed facts of the case demonstrate that Ms. Yoder's conduct was not authorized, was not foreseeable, was not in the furtherance of its business or interests, and arose wholly from an external, independent motive.

"A genuine issue [of material fact] exists where the record contains competent material that evidences two plausible, but contradictory, accounts of the essential facts. A genuine issue is a dispute that is real, not merely argumentative, imaginary, or frivolous." *Rustco Prods. Co. v. Food Corn, Inc.*, 925 S.W.2d 917, 922–23 (Mo.App. W.D.1996) (internal quotation marks and citation omitted). "Under the doctrine of respondeat superior, an employer is held responsible for the misconduct of an employee where that employee is acting within the course and scope of his employment." *Tuttle v. Muenks*, 964 S.W.2d 514, 517 (Mo.App. W.D.1998). The employer can be held liable despite the absence of any negligence on its part. *Id.* "If reasonable minds could differ on the question of whether an employee was acting within scope and course of his or her employment, then the question is one of fact to be settled by jury." *Id.*

Allee's claims that it was entitled to summary judgment as a matter of law because the undisputed facts show that Allee's did not authorize Ms. Yoder to place the toothpick in the drink. However, an employer is liable for an employee's torts even if the employer did not authorize the employee's conduct as long as "the employee committed such act while engaged in an activity falling within the scope of the employee's authority or employment." *P.S. v. Psychiatric Coverage, Ltd.*, 887 S.W.2d 622, 624 (Mo.App. E.D.1994). Thus, summary judgment based on a lack of authorization is improper because whether the act of putting the toothpick in the beer was authorized is immaterial to whether Allees can be found liable.

The course and scope of employment is defined "as acts (1) which, even though not specifically authorized, are done to further the business or interests of the employer under his 'general authority and direction' and (2) which **naturally** arise from the performance of the employer's work." *Maryland Cas. Co. v. Huger*, 728 S.W.2d 574, 579 (Mo.App. E.D.1987) (emphasis added). " '**[N]aturally**,' implies that the employees' conduct must be usual, customary and expected. This amounts to a requirement of foreseeability." *Id.* at 579–80 (emphasis added).

Allee's argued in its summary judgment motion that Ms. Yoder's action of placing a toothpick in a beer was not foreseeable and not in furtherance of its business or interests and, thus, was outside the scope of her employment. Specifically, Allee's argues that the battery must naturally arise from the performance of Ms. Yoder's work and placing a toothpick in beer does not naturally arise from proper bartendering. Allee's has confused what must be foreseen here. It is clear from *P.S.* that respondeat superior applies to torts committed "while [the employee is] engaged in an activity" that is within the scope of employment. 887 S.W.2d at 624. The conduct causing the tort must naturally arise from the employee's work. In this case, a jury could determine that Ms. Yoder's conduct naturally arose from bartendering because she committed a tort—placing a toothpick in the beer—while she was engaged in an activity—serving a beer—that was usual, customary, and expected of a bartender.

Moreover, a bartender serving a beer to a customer could be considered conduct in furtherance of Allee's interest and, thus, within the scope of employment. Contrary to Allee's argument, Ms. Yoder's subjective belief that she did not act in furtherance of Allee's interests or business is not a statement of fact but a conclusion of law that a trial court "should disregard in ruling on a motion for summary judgment." *Zerebco v. Lolli Bros. Livestock Mkt.*, 918 S.W.2d 931, 934 (Mo.App. W.D.1996). Thus, her testimony does not dispose of the issue of whether her conduct—serving a beer knowing a toothpick was in it—was within the scope of her employment.

   . . .

## Conclusion

For the foregoing reasons, we reverse and remand for further proceedings.

SMART, P.J., and HOLLIGER, J., concur.

## Exercise 7   Auto burglary (United States)

This is the final set of exercises of the whole book! It is time to try to use all the skills you have been practicing in a way that mimics the types of things you will be required to do if pursuing legal studies in an English-speaking jurisdiction.

In order to be able to write IRAC answers to the hypos below, you will need to closely read the relevant statute and identify its key elements; closely read the cases related to the crime as defined by the statute, analyzing the legal issue, the key facts, and how the court interprets both the statute and other cases relevant to it in coming to its judgment; identify how the law has developed as the cases are decided; and work out how certain cases can be distinguished from others depending on the key facts in issue. You will then need to analyze each hypo in the exercises and, having considered each case, work out which ones are relevant to the facts at issue in the hypo. Finally, when you have done all these tasks, you will be able to plan out a response answering the question in each hypo and then write out a full answer using the IRAC structure.

This approach to answering the legal questions replicates exactly how you will be expected to put together answers during such things as LL.M. courses. Therefore, we have deliberately left the final exercises less structured so that you can practice gathering together all the information and sifting through which bits are useful to you in coming up with an answer. That is, after all, exactly what lawyers do every day.

Even if you are not intending to pursue further academic qualifications, by adopting the skills and organizational structures you have been practicing, you will find that in a common law setting, you are much more effective in putting together such things as legal memos for clients. In fact, we, as the authors, believe that even if you never come into contact with the common law, by training yourself to think in the ways you have been practicing using this book, you will be a better lawyer overall, whatever jurisdiction you find yourself in.

### Lead-in

The following exercises all relate to the crime of burglary of a vehicle in the state of California (you can choose to do all or just a few). You will notice when you read the cases that follow that there are various issues relating to this crime in California, which are not immediately obvious from just reading the statute. As we outlined in previous chapters, this is exactly how the common law works, with case law filling out, clarifying, and even moderating the law set out in the original statute. Unlike with many of the previous exercises in the book, for these final exercises we are not giving you clues to key vocabulary or questions that may help you identify important things, such as the legal issues. This is a chance for you to practice, in a much more realistic way, some of the key skills we have been helping you develop.

For each hypothetical situation, refer to the relevant statute and to the cases that appear below. You will find that some cases are more relevant to each hypo than others, but deciding this is part of the analytical process of being a lawyer. Once you have decided which cases are relevant to each hypo, come to a conclusion for each of them whether there has been a burglary. Finally, set out your analysis for each hypo using any variation on the IRAC form.

### Hypo 1

Bob sees a car parked on the street in a city in California. He uses a screwdriver to force open the locked hood. He steals the battery.

### Hypo 2

Murat broke a car window, reached in, and took a package from the passenger's seat. All the car doors were locked. However, the trunk had been left unlocked. Due to the design of the car, it would have been possible for someone to open the trunk and enter the passenger compartment by pushing down the back seat. Murat did not know this.

### Hypo 3

Carmen drove a delivery truck for Heavenly Bakeries. After making her morning deliveries, she decided to get lunch. She parked the truck in the restaurant parking lot and locked both doors to the passenger compartment.

The cargo portion of the truck had to be locked separately, using an external padlock. Unfortunately, Carmen had left the lock back at the bakery. However, she found some rope in the truck. Carmen threaded the rope through the holes where the padlock was supposed to go, and tied the best knot that she could. Then she went inside to eat.

While Carmen was in the restaurant, Alex came by and saw that the back of the truck was only secured with a rope. Alex, who had been a sailor before turning to a life of crime, had no trouble untying Carmen's knot—though it might have been difficult for someone else. He entered the cargo portion of the truck and took as much fresh bread as he could carry. Unfortunately for him, a police officer who happened to be passing by caught him.

## Hypo 4

Lou parked his car on the street. When he left the car, the windows were rolled up, and both the doors and trunk were closed. The door locks, however, were broken so that they could not be locked.

The trunk lock, on the other hand, was broken in such a way that it locked each time it was closed. Not only that, it could not be opened from the outside with a key. To access the trunk, one had to pull a lever located inside the passenger compartment. To reach the lever, the driver's door had to be open. Lou did not keep anything of value in the passenger compartment of his car, but he did have golf clubs in the trunk.

Alicia opened the unlocked driver's door and opened the trunk by pulling the lever. She took the golf clubs and walked off.

## Hypo 5

Herb had a van, and he locked all of the doors when he parked it in front of his house. However, the lock on the double back doors was a bit "loose" and did not work perfectly. He knew that if a person pulled really hard they might be able to open them. He also knew that the lock had another problem: it was sometimes possible to unlock it with a key roughly the same size and shape as the correct one.

One night, Herb looked out his window and saw a large man near the van. The man, Ross, gave a hard pull on the rear doors to open them and crawled in. Herb called the police. Then he ran down, restrained Ross, and held him until the police arrived. When police searched Ross, they did not find any keys or any burglar tools on him. When one of the officers—a man of average height and weight—locked the doors again and tried to pull them open them himself, he was unable to do so.

## Hypo 6

Katy drives her jeep to the beach and leaves it in the public parking lot. Although the top is down, out of habit, she locks all the doors. She hides her expensive watch in the glove compartment, which she also locks. However, the latch of the glove compartment is slightly broken, and it is possible to force it open if pulled hard enough. She forgets that she has left her work mobile phone on the back seat of the jeep.

Jonny sees Katy walking away from the jeep and decides to see whether she has left anything that he can quickly steal. He walks to the vehicle and immediately sees the phone on the back seat. He leans over and grabs it. Seeing nothing else, he climbs into the jeep to check the glove box. He sees that the door of the glove box looks a bit loose, and he pulls it hard, causing it to open. He sees the watch and takes it.

## Hypo 7

The same facts as in exercise 6, but in this case the glove compartment door is not broken, and Jonny has to open it using a screwdriver.

## Hypo 8

An exclusive restaurant uses a valet service for its customers. When the valets are distracted, Wanda manages to take the electronic key to an expensive luxury car. She is able to quickly clone it.

Before the owner finishes dinner and returns for the car, Wanda unlocks the car with the cloned key and steals a laptop and an expensive camera from the back seat.

## Hypo 9

Barney parks his convertible in a car park, locks it, and goes to a movie theater. Jake notices there is a small tear in the fabric of the roof, just large enough for him to insert his arm inside the car and steal a mobile phone, which is sitting on one of the seats.

## Hypo 10

Milt opens the gas cap of a large RV. There is no door over the gas cap, and the cap itself cannot be locked. After Milt opens it, he extracts a full tank of gas.

## California legal authorities

### Statute

*West's Ann. Cal. Penal Code § 459*
Every person who enters any . . . vehicle . . . when the doors are locked . . . with intent to commit grand or petit larceny or any felony is guilty of burglary.

*Cases*

148 Cal.App.2d 465, 306 P.2d 953
District Court of Appeal, Second District, Division 3, California.
The PEOPLE of the State of California, Plaintiff and Appellant,

v.

John H. TOOMES and Philander Smith, Defendants and Respondents.
Feb. 11, 1957.

SHINN, Presiding Justice.

John H. Toomes and Philander Smith were accused of burglary and upon the preliminary hearing were committed for trial. They made a motion to set aside the information under section 995 of the Penal Code upon the ground that they had been committed without reasonable or probable cause. The motion was granted and the People appeal.

The evidence at the preliminary hearing established the following facts: Harry Bergerson parked his automobile on the street. He closed the windows and locked the doors. The trunk was locked. Defendants drove up in a car, parked alongside, opened the trunk with a tire iron rim and screw driver and took therefrom a spare tire mounted on a rim. They were later apprehended with the rim and tire in question, and two others, in the trunk of their car and were placed under arrest.

The question on appeal is whether the defendants were guilty of burglary or only of theft. Section 459 of the Penal Code provides in part: "Every person who enters any . . . vehicle as defined by said code when the doors of such vehicle are locked . . . with intent to commit grand or petit larceny or any felony is guilty of burglary." An automobile is such a vehicle. § 31, Vehicle Code. It is the contention of defendants, which prevailed in the trial court, that the words, "the doors of such vehicle are locked" refer only to the side doors of an automobile and cannot reasonably be understood as including the cover of the trunk. Therefore, they argue that in order to constitute burglary there must be an unlawful entry into the section of the car that is entered through the side doors. They concede that if the lid or cover of a trunk is one of the doors of the vehicle within the meaning of section 459, and is locked, an entry into the trunk compartment for the purpose of committing a theft would constitute burglary. "Door" is defined in Webster's New International Dictionary, Second Edition, Unabridged: "1. The movable frame or barrier of boards, or other material, usually turning on hinges or pivots or sliding, by which an entranceway into a house or apartment is closed and opened; also, a similar part of a piece of furniture, as in a cabinet or bookcase. 2. An opening in the wall of a house or of an apartment, by which to go in and out; an entranceway; a doorway. 3. Passage; means of approach or access."

In deciding whether it was the intent of the legislature in using the word "doors" that it should include only the side doors of a vehicle or also the lid or cover of the trunk, a most satisfactory guide to the legislative intention would be the apparent evils sought to be prevented, namely, the breaking into the interior sections of locked cars. Manifestly, making the offense a felony would tend to minimize the frequency of such unlawful acts. It is apparent that that purpose could not be adequately accomplished by denouncing as a felony entry by the breaking or opening of locks of the side doors without also making it an equally serious offense to enter a locked trunk compartment for the purpose of committing theft. The trunks or luggage compartments of automobiles are fitted with locks for the very reason that they furnish a convenient place for the carrying of things of value. We think the word "door" better describes the top of a luggage compartment than would any of the words "top," "cover," or "lid." We do not associate hinges and locks with such coverings, but we do associate them with doors. And we have always understood that the entrance to a cellar is through a cellar door, even though it may lift upward instead of outward. There are, of course, many types of doors to small compartments, such as cupboard doors, which are entered only by reaching into them. There is room for difference of opinion whether the cover of a luggage compartment would generally be included in the term "doors" but we believe any doubts as to the meaning to be given it in construing the statute is removed when effect is given to the purpose of the statute, namely, to make it a more serious offense to break into the interior of a car than to merely steal something from it. We are therefore of the opinion that the act of entering the trunk of an automobile for the purpose of theft, when the door of the trunk and all other doors are locked is burglary. That is the only question for decision.

The order is reversed.

. . .

20 Cal.App.3d 1078, 98 Cal.Rptr. 231
THE PEOPLE, Plaintiff and Respondent,

v.

JERRY LAVON BLALOCK, Defendant and
Appellant
Crim. No. 19915.
Court of Appeal, Second District, Division 4, California.
November 8, 1971.

JEFFERSON, Acting P. J.

A jury found defendant guilty of second degree burglary as charged in count IV of an amended information. . . . A motion for a new trial and probation was denied and defendant was committed to California Youth Authority. Defendant appeals from the judgment of conviction.

On October 20, 1970, Miss Thomas was the owner of a 1959 Pontiac automobile which she parked on Imperial Highway near Compton Avenue [and when she came back, the car was gone].

In the trunk, which was locked, she had a red bumper jack, some mechanical tools and two tool boxes, one large one and a small red tool box. The trunk of the vehicle was locked and could be opened only with a screwdriver; the key would not unlock it.

. . .

On October 21 Frank Oliphante was on his job at 92d and Graham Streets near Beach. He observed a 1959 Pontiac which was parked nearby and noticed the defendant and another man standing near the rear of the Pontiac. He also observed that one of the men opened the trunk of the Pontiac with what appeared to be a screwdriver. The defendant and the other person removed the red tool box from the trunk of the car and carried it down an alley and put it on the ground behind a building. They returned to the Pontiac and removed the other tool box and put it on the ground near the first tool box. They lifted the jack out of the trunk and put it on the ground.

Jack Reidy of the Los Angeles Police Department was patrolling eastbound on 92d Street near Beach in a police vehicle. Frank Oliphante told the officer what he had observed . . . .

Officer Reidy arrested defendant and advised him of his constitutional rights.

. . .

. . . Defendant urges that the court should have . . . given the jury the following instruction: "In order to constitute auto burglary, all the doors and the trunk of an automobile must have been locked." Although, in [*People v. Toomes*, 148 Cal.App.2d 465], the evidence showed that the passenger doors, as well as the trunk door, were locked and the last sentences of that opinion refer to that factual situation, we cannot read *Toomes* as standing only for the limited meaning defendant ascribes to it. It would be ridiculous to make the existence of burglary turn on the locked or unlocked state of an area not involved in the entry. If the entry is made by unlocking the trunk door, it is immaterial that some other door, leading to some other space, was unlocked.

. . .

The judgment of conviction is affirmed.

. . .

47 Cal.App.3d 217, 120 Cal.Rptr. 667
Court of Appeal, Third District, California.
The PEOPLE of the State of California, Plaintiff and Appellant,
v.
Claude William MALCOLM, Defendant and Respondent.
Cr. 7767.
April 15, 1975.

Rehearing Denied April 29, 1975.
Hearing Denied June 11, 1975.
REGAN, Associate Justice.

By an information filed on October 10, 1973, the defendant Malcolm was accused of violating Penal Code section 459, burglary of a locked automobile. Upon a Penal Code section 995 defense motion, the trial court granted a dismissal of the charge on the basis the car was not locked at the time of the alleged offense. (See Pen.Code, s 1385.) The People appeal from the dismissal.

On June 30, 1973, at approximately 9:30 a.m., Arthur Armstrong drove with some friends to a spot on the Cache Creek in Yolo County, parked his car near the creek and locked all the doors of his Volkswagen with a key. All the car windows were rolled up and closed. However, the left front wing lock was broken preventing it from being locked. The group then left.

. . .

[Officer Beal observed Malcolm and another man named Stiles approach the Volkswagen.]

. . .

When Stiles came to Armstrong's Volkswagen, he first tried both doors. On the driver's side of the car Officer Beal observed Stiles open the wind wing, reach his arm inside and open the door. Stiles then entered the car, checked out various items of property, and exited the car with an armload of property. The defendant Malcolm approached the car and also carried some objects from it . . . . At this point the officers approached the three men and placed them under arrest.

Officer Beal examined the wing window after the arrest. He testified that there were signs of forced entry. The wind wing was broken, the latch on the wind wing was broken, and there were smudge marks on the window indicating where pressure had been applied to the wind wing.

Section 459 of the Penal Code provides, in pertinent part, as follows: "Every person who enters any . . . vehicle as defined by said (Vehicle) code when the doors of such vehicle are locked, . . . with intent to commit grand or petit larceny or any felony is guilty of burglary."

The Attorney General contends that auto burglary is established by proof of an unauthorized entry into an automobile through locked doors and closed windows with intent to steal and therefore the trial court erred in dismissing the charge.

The Attorney General argues the available legal authorities support the spirit, if not the letter, of his position. He initially relies upon *People v. Toomes* (1957) 148 Cal.App. 2d 465, 306 P. 2d 953.

In *Toomes* the evidence disclosed that the owner of a car parked his car, closed the windows and locked the doors. The trunk was locked. Subsequently, the defendants opened the trunk with a tire iron and screw driver and took a spare tire. On a People's appeal from the granting of a Penal Code section 995 motion, the defendants contended that a locked trunk was not a locked door within the meaning of Penal Code section 459. In reversing the trial court's order, the Court of Appeal looked to legislative intent, stating (at p. 466, 306 P. 2d at p. 954):

"In deciding whether it was the intent of the Legislature in using the word 'doors' that it should include only the side doors of a vehicle or also the lid or cover of the trunk, a most satisfactory guide to the legislative intention would be the apparent evils sought to be prevented, namely, the breaking into the interior sections of locked cars. Manifestly, making the offense a felony would tend to minimize the frequency of such unlawful acts. It is apparent that that purpose could not be adequately accomplished by denouncing as a felony entry by the breaking or opening of locks of the side doors without also making it an equally serious offense to enter a locked trunk compartment for the purpose of committing theft. The trunks or luggage compartments of automobiles are fitted with locks for the very reason that they furnish a convenient place for the carrying of things of value."

The court then concluded (at p. 467, 306 P. 2d at p. 954):

"There is room for difference of opinion whether the cover of a luggage compartment would generally be included in the term 'doors' but we believe any doubts as to the meaning to be given it in construing the statute is removed when effect is given to the purpose of the statute, namely, to make it a more serious offense to break into the interior of a car than to merely steal something from it. We are therefore of the opinion that the act of entering the trunk of an automobile for the purpose of theft, when the door of the trunk and all other doors are locked is burglary."

. . .

. . . [T]he Attorney General contends the auto burglary statute should be construed flexibly with the principal objective of discouraging the social evil which that statute was designed to prevent. . . .

. . .

Defendant sets forth a three-pronged argument: He first contends the statute must be interpreted literally, i.e., the door was not locked since the wind wing could be opened. Secondly, he argues that the statute, by necessary implication, requires a "breaking," and that element is missing here. Finally, defendant argues that it is the policy of this state to construe a penal statute as favorably to the defendant as its language and circumstances reasonably permit. (See *Keeler v. Superior Court* (1970) 2 Cal.3d 619, 631, 87 Cal.Rptr. 481, 470 P.2d 617.)

We are here presented with an anomalous situation, one which the Legislature surely did not anticipate. For all intents and purposes the car in question was locked. By mere happenstance, one wind [wing] was faulty and could not be tightly secured, thereby allowing the defendant to gain entrance into the car.

A literal reading of the statute supports the defendant's view. However, we decline to accept the defendant's position since we are persuaded by the Attorney General's principal argument.

We have concluded the import of *Toomes* . . . is that common sense construction must be used in interpreting Penal Code section 459. We are convinced that the auto burglary statute should be construed flexibly with the principal objective of discouraging the social evil which that statute was designed to prevent. . . . Accordingly, we hold that, under the facts of this case, auto burglary was established, and therefore the trial court erred.

The order dismissing the Penal Code section 459 charge against defendant is reversed.

PUGLIA, P.J., and EVANS, J., concur.

112 Cal.App.3d 226, 169 Cal.Rptr. 179

Court of Appeal, First District, Division 2,

California.

PEOPLE of the State of California, Plaintiff and Appellant,

v.

German WOODS, Jr., Defendant and Respondent.

Cr. 20689.

Nov. 18, 1980.

As Modified Dec. 11, 1980.

TAYLOR, Presiding Justice.

The People appeal from a judgment granting defendant's Penal Code section 995 motion to dismiss the first count of the information, which charged him with a burglary of a vehicle (Pen. Code, s 459). The only question on appeal is whether the court below properly concluded that the People had failed to prove an essential element of the offense as defendant entered a vehicle whose doors were locked by reaching into a window that had been left open deliberately. For the reasons set forth below, we have concluded that the judgment must be affirmed.

The pertinent facts as established by the transcript of the preliminary hearing are as follows: On September 22, 1979, as part of a decoy operation, Officer David Fontana of the San Francisco Police Department, placed a coin purse containing $3 and a Pentax camera on the passenger seat of his private automobile, a 1978 Volkswagen. The bills and the camera were marked. Fontana parked the vehicle in a parking lot, locked the doors and rolled up all the windows except for the passenger window which was rolled down approximately five and one-half inches. He did so to provide an exact measure for his testimony and to prevent any damage to his car. Fontana then walked across the street and staked out the car, along with his partner Officer Collins. Both had an unobstructed view. They saw defendant walk towards the car, stop, look around, and then reach in through the passenger window of the vehicle and remove the purse. After emptying the purse, defendant discarded it and then returned to Fontana's car and reached through the window to remove the camera. Defendant was apprehended immediately.

So far as here pertinent, Penal Code section 459 provides: "Every person who enters any . . . vehicle . . . when the doors of such vehicle are locked, . . . with intent to commit grand or petit larceny or any felony is guilty of burglary . . ."

The question is whether the trial court properly concluded that the partially open window prevented the car from being "locked," within the meaning of the statute, as quoted above. The People argue that under a strict construction of the statute, the partially open window was irrelevant, as all of the elements of the offense were satisfied once the People had established that the doors were locked.

Generally, this state has defined burglary as entry with the requisite intent, as the common law element of breaking has never been an essential element of the offense (*People v. Allison*, 200 Cal. 404, 408, 253 P. 318; Criminal Law-Development of the Law of Burglary in Cal., 25 Santa Clara L.Rev. 74, 85). However, where the place entered is a vehicle, the Legislature added another element to the corpus delicti, namely, that the doors of the vehicle "are locked." Thus, where there is no evidence that the doors were locked, although there was broken glass, the elements of the offense are not established (*People v. Burns*, 114 Cal.App.2d 566, 250 P.2d 619). The People's argument overlooks the fact that the statute consistently has been construed in a liberal and common sense manner.

In *People v. Toomes*, 148 Cal.App. 2d 465, 306 P. 2d 953, the court held that the lid of an automobile trunk was a "door," within the meaning of the statute. The court reached its conclusion, after an analysis, that "... a most satisfactory guide to the legislative intention would be the apparent evils sought to be prevented, namely, the breaking into the interior sections of locked cars." (*Toomes*, supra, p. 466; emphasis added.) The *Toomes* court further noted at page 467 that the purpose of the statute was to "... make it a more serious offense to break into the interior of a car than to merely steal something from it." (Emphasis added).

. . .

The trial court here relied on *People v. Malcolm*, 47 Cal.App.3d 217, 120 Cal.Rptr. 667 ... to hold, at page 223, 120 Cal.Rptr. 667, that the "mere happenstance" of a broken wind wing latch of an otherwise locked vehicle did not preclude the application of the statute, as for "all intents and purposes the car in question was locked." ... The "mere happenstance" that prevented the vehicle from being tightly secured in Malcolm is patently absent in the case at bench. Fontana's uncontroverted testimony indicates his deliberate intent to maintain an aperture of five and one-half inches to prevent any damage to his vehicle and to provide a basis for his testimony. Only an absurd interpretation of the statute would permit such an evasion of the requirement that the entire vehicle be secured insofar as possible. . . .

. . .

We conclude, therefore, that the judgment must be and is affirmed.

241 Cal.App.2d 812, 51 Cal.Rptr. 18
THE PEOPLE, Plaintiff and Respondent,
v.
CECIL MASSIE, Defendant and Appellant.
District Court of Appeal, Second District, Division 1, California.
May 4, 1966.

WOOD, P. J.

In an amended information the defendant was accused of burglary in that he willfully entered a vehicle . . . the doors of said vehicle being locked, and with the intent then and there to commit theft.

In a jury trial, defendant was found guilty of burglary in the first degree. Probation was denied, and he was sentenced to imprisonment in the state prison. He appeals from the judgment.

. . .

Appellant contends (as shown by his briefs on the original hearing) that the court did not instruct the jury properly . . . .

On December 3, 1963, about 10 p.m., Mr. Collier, a truck driver in the employ of the Thrifty Drug Company, drove a truck-tractor, to which were attached two 22-foot semitrailers, containing drug store merchandise, to a place at the rear of a Thrifty Drug Store in Compton and parked the vehicle there. . . .

The first trailer (the one next to the tractor) had a double-door at the rear end and a single door on each side. Each of the doors on this trailer was sealed by a metal clip, which is a piece or strip of pliable metal about six inches long, and one-fourth inch wide, which "goes around the hasp over the handle of the door"—and one end of the strip is placed through a clip at the other end of the strip, and then the clip locks itself. When the doors are sealed with a clip, it is necessary to use force to break the metal seal in order to open the doors.

The second or rear trailer had a rear door and a side door, which doors were locked with devices or padlocks which could be opened only by using a key.

. . . The assistant manager Mr. Banks, after obtaining the key to the trailer, proceeded with Mr. Collier and another employee, Mr. Collado, to the trailers. As they approached the trailers, they saw the defendant Massie standing inside the first trailer and they saw another man, who was outside that trailer, holding the side door of the trailer open. The metal seal on that door had been broken. Then the man who was holding the door ran away. The defendant jumped out of the trailer and started walking away. . . . Then two police officers, who were on patrol duty, arrived there in a police car and arrested defendant.

. . .

Appellant contends that the court erred in giving the following two instructions: (1) ". . . that the word 'lock' means to make fast by the inter-linking or interlacing of parts." (2) "If you find as a matter of fact that all the doors of the semi-trailer were secured with metal seals such as Exhibit No. 1 in evidence prior to the entry, and that application of some force was required to break the seal to permit entry to the interior of the vehicle through the door, then such vehicle was locked within the meaning of the law." Appellant argues that these are instructions on questions of fact, and that they instruct the jury that a seal is a lock. Section 459 of the Penal Code provides, in part: "Every person who enters any house . . . or other building . . . trailer coach as defined by the Vehicle Code, vehicle as defined by said code *when the doors of such vehicle are locked,* . . . with intent to commit . . . larceny or any felony is guilty of burglary." (Italics added.) In the present case, the evidence was uncontradicted that, when the driver entered the store, each door of the first trailer was sealed with a pliable metal strip "around the hasp over the handle of the door," with one end of the strip through a self-locking clip at the other end of the strip. The definition of the word "lock," as stated in the given instruction, was a correct definition of that word. The other instruction, above quoted, was to the effect that if the jury found as a matter of fact that all the doors of the semitrailer (first trailer) were secured with metal seals, as described in the evidence, the vehicle was locked within the meaning of said code section. The matter of construing the section was a question of law for the court. It does not appear that the court instructed the jury as to what the facts were with respect to questions of fact. It appears that the court was instructing the jury that if it found certain facts, then and in that event the court was declaring as a matter of law that the trailer was a locked vehicle within the meaning of said code section. Under the evidence, it was proper to instruct the jury that the trailer was locked.

. . .

The judgment is affirmed.

. . .

245 Cal.Rptr. 870
200 Cal.App.3d 244
In re LAMONT R., a Person Coming Under the Juvenile Court Law.
The PEOPLE, Plaintiff and Respondent,
v.
LAMONT R., Defendant and Appellant.
No. A037522.
Court of Appeal, First District, Division 2, California.
April 14, 1988.

SMITH, Associate Justice.

In 1985, Lamont R. was judged to be a ward of the court and was ordered to comply with the terms of a home probation contract (Welf. & Inst.Code, § 602). On July 15, 1986, petitions were filed charging Lamont with attempted vehicular burglary and requesting that the prior probation order be modified (Pen.Code, §§ 459, 664; Welf. & Inst.Code, § 777, subd. (a)). After denying a motion to dismiss for insufficient evidence, the court found the allegations to be true beyond a reasonable doubt. Appellant appeals from the finding and subsequent disposition order.

## BACKGROUND

David Worley testified that on the evening of July 11, 1986, he parked a Santa Fe trailer loaded with cases of wine on 98th Avenue in Oakland, and drove away in the cab. The rear trailer doors were locked with a master padlock and fastened with a metal shipment seal. The door handles pass over an eyebolt; a lock and shipment seal were fastened through the eyebolt. The shipment seal was secured through the eyebolt after the truck was fully loaded, and the doors could not be opened unless the seal was cut off or broken. The seal cannot be unfastened and later resealed.

At 11:56 p.m. on July 12, 1986, Officer Fausto Melara arrived at the trailer to investigate a reported burglary. He found the rear doors of the trailer open and observed that the contents had been disturbed. He found a broken shipment seal inside the truck but did not find any lock. Officer Melara closed the doors and latched them at top and bottom. He closed the swivel that goes over the latches. He then secured the doors with two chains that were fixed to the center of each door. Each chain had a hook at its end. Officer Melara wrapped the chains around each other and hooked them into the hooks on opposite sides of the doors. He then directed a police dispatcher to send for a tow truck and waited in his patrol car approximately 150 feet away.

About an hour later Officer Melara observed appellant and another male walking southbound on 98th Avenue. They walked past the trailer, looked around, and then returned to the rear doors. Appellant and his companion unhooked the chains, unfastened the latches and pulled open at least one door. Officer Melara testified that "just as it looked at that time that the [appellant] was about to climb in, [a] truck came." Apparently startled by the oncoming truck, appellant slammed the door shut and walked away. Officer Melara took both boys into custody.

## APPEAL

. . . The only issue therefore is whether the trailer was locked within the meaning of section 459. The facts are not in dispute and the question appears to be one of law. . . .

Section 459 provides, in part: "Every person who enters any house, . . . [or] vehicle as defined by the Vehicle Code when the doors are locked . . . with intent to commit grand or petit larceny or any felony is guilty of burglary." (Emphasis added.) An essential element of vehicular burglary under this section is that the vehicle must be locked. (*People v. Woods* (1980) 112 Cal.App.3d 226, 230, 169 Cal.Rptr. 179; *In re Charles G.* (1979) 95 Cal.App.3d 62, 65, 156 Cal. Rptr. 832.) " '[T]he word 'lock' means to make fast by the interlinking or interlacing of parts . . . [such that] some force [is] required to break the seal to permit entry. . . . '" (*People v. Massie*, supra, 241 Cal.App.2d at p. 817, 51 Cal.Rptr. 18, approving of an instruction.) The Oxford English Dictionary defines "lock" as "1. An appliance for fastening a door, lid, etc., consisting of a bolt (or system of bolts) with mechanism by which it can be propelled and withdrawn by means of a key or similar instrument." (VI Oxford English Dict. (1978) p. 383.)

The uncontroverted testimony shows that the doors were locked and sealed when Mr. Worley left the van on July 11. By the time Officer Melara appeared on the scene, the shipment seal was broken and the padlock removed by persons unknown. Since there was no way to lock the doors,

Melara closed the doors, wrapped two chains around each other and hooked them into opposite bolts. No force was needed, no seals were broken to gain entry. Appellant simply unhooked the chains, unfastened the latches, and pulled open the door.

The language of section 459 shows that the Legislature intended it to be a more serious crime to enter a locked vehicle than an unlocked one. The crime of burglary is committed when a person, with the requisite intent, enters a dwelling or a defined class of vehicles, whether locked or unlocked. But the Legislature specifically required locking as an essential element of common vehicular burglary. We would do violence to this relatively clear statutory directive if we were to find that the chain and hook contraption improvised by Officer Melara constituted a lock. A door held shut with masking tape would have been just as easy to open.

The attorney general relies on *People v. Malcolm* (1975) 47 Cal.App.3d 217, 120 Cal.Rptr. 667. In *Malcolm*, an automobile was left parked with all its windows closed and all its doors locked. One wing window, although closed, had a broken latch. The defendant forced open the wing window, reached inside and unlocked the door. The car was deemed locked. The court stated, "For all intents and purposes the car in question was locked. By mere happenstance, one wind wing was faulty and could not be tightly secured. . . ." (*Id.*, at p. 223, 120 Cal.Rptr. 667.)

*Malcolm* is distinguishable from the present case. In *Malcolm*, there was evidence of forced entry: "The wind wing was broken, the latch on the wind wing was broken, and there were smudge marks on the window indicating where pressure had been applied to the wind wing." (*Id.*, at p. 220, 120 Cal. Rptr. 667.) Having achieved forced entry into the interior of the vehicle, the defendant then reached in and disengaged the locking mechanism which secured the doors. (*Id.*, at p. 219, 120 Cal.Rptr. 667.) The court concluded that a "common sense construction" of the statute dictated that the defendant's conduct fell within the evil which the Legislature sought to prevent. (*Id.*, at p. 223, 120 Cal.Rptr. 667.) By contrast, appellant used no pressure; he broke no seal; he disengaged no mechanism that could reasonably be called a lock. The attorney general also argues that "locked" should be construed to mean "secured insofar as possible," and that Officer Melara's conduct met this test. We reject this argument. If such were the case any car door or trunk without a functioning lock would be deemed "locked" merely by the owner's act of closing it. Such an interpretation is clearly inconsistent with the Legislature's intent that unauthorized entry into a locked vehicle be deemed a more serious crime than unauthorized entry of one that is not locked. . . .

. . .

## DISPOSITION

The findings and disposition order appealed from are reversed.
KLINE, P.J., and ROUSE, J., concur.


## Conclusion

First, if you have got to this part of the book having done most of the exercises, congratulations! Writing IRAC answers, in particular, is often very challenging at first for students, but as they say, practice makes perfect. Even if you don't feel you can do it all quite perfectly just yet, you have definitely given yourself a better chance of being more successful in your continuing legal studies if you have worked through the statutes and cases and written an answer to the hypos in this chapter.

In addition to using some of the skills you first encountered in chapters 1 and 2, you have also practiced the following:

- Identifying each component of the IRAC structure (and/or one of its variants) in a written legal response.
- Identifying and analyzing the key legal issue(s) presented in a hypothetical scenario.
- Identifying relevant statutes and/or cases to address the legal issue in a hypothetical scenario.
- Applying legal principles to the facts of a hypothetical scenario.
- Incorporating references to statutes and/or cases in written answers to legal problems written using an IRAC-style structure.
- Constructing a coherent and accurately written response to a legal problem using appropriate legal terminology in an IRAC-style structure.

Wherever your legal journey takes you from now on, the skills you have started to develop using this book will ease your path.

# Notes

## Introduction

1. Common law is the system of law that developed in England in the premodern era and which is generally now practiced in English-speaking jurisdictions or former British colonies, including the United States, Canada, India, and Australia.

2. For theoretical support for this insight, see, for example, Jill J. Ramsfield, "Is 'Logic' Culturally Based? A Contrastive, International Approach to the U.S. Law Classroom," *Journal of Legal Education* 47, no. 2 (1997); Diane B. Kraft, "Contrastive Analysis and Contrastive Rhetoric in the Legal Writing Classroom," *New Mexico Law Review* 49, no. 1 (Winter 2019): 35–58.

3. For the importance of the study of legal writing and legal analysis, see Julie M. Spanbauer, "Lost in Translation in the Law School Classroom: Assessing Required Coursework in LL.M. Programs for International Students," *International Journal of Legal Information* 35, no. 3 (2007): 396–446.

## Chapter 1

1. You can find a brief guide to some of these principles from the following source: Georgetown Law, *A Guide to Reading, Interpreting and Applying Statutes*, https://www.law.georgetown.edu/wp-content/uploads/2018/12/A-Guide-to-Reading-Interpreting-and-Applying-Statutes-1.pdf, accessed November 21, 2023. Further summaries of methods of statutory interpretation can be found in John C. Dernbach et al., *A Practical Guide to Legal Writing and Legal Method*, 7th ed. (Aspen Publishing, 2021), 133–143. See also Jeffrey A. Pojanowski, "Reading Statutes in the Common Law Tradition," *Virginia Law Review* 101, no. 5 (September 2015): 1357–1424 for a discussion on different approaches that can be taken to reading and interpreting statutes.

2. Andrei Marmor, *The Language of Law* (Oxford University Press, 2014).

3. The statutes in this section were influenced by NJ Rev Stat § 2A:22A-5 (2022).

4. Crown Copyright 2013. Contains public sector information licensed under the Open Government Licence v3.0. https://www.nationalarchives.gov.uk/doc/open-government-licence/version/3/.

5. These materials contain information that has been derived from information originally made available by the Province of British Columbia at http://www.bclaws.gov.bc.ca, and this information is being used in accordance with the King's Printer Licence – British Columbia available at https://www.bclaws.gov.bc.ca/standards/Licence.html. They have not, however, been produced in affiliation with, or with the endorsement of, the Province of British Columbia, and THESE MATERIALS ARE NOT AN OFFICIAL VERSION.

6. Crown Copyright 1984. Contains public sector information licensed under the Open Government Licence v3.0. https://www.nationalarchives.gov.uk/doc/open-government-licence/version/3/.

7. Exercise 5 was inspired by a series of exercises in Debra Suzette Lee, Charles Hall, and Susan M. Barone, *American Legal English: Using Language in Legal Contexts*, 2nd ed. (University of Michigan Press, 2007), 62–65.

8. Copyright © State of New South Wales. Sourced from the New South Wales Legislation website on November 21, 2023. For the latest information on New South Wales Government legislation, see https://www.legislation.nsw.gov.au.

9. The authors have diligently attempted to ensure that the Criminal Code of Canada sections reproduced in this exercise are accurate. However, they are reproduced here for educational use only; they do not represent legal advice, nor should they be used as a resource for anyone providing legal advice. Their inclusion here does not represent the endorsement of any government body, and THESE MATERIALS ARE NOT AN OFFICIAL VERSION.

10. Copyright © State of New South Wales. Sourced from the New South Wales Legislation website on November 21, 2023. For the latest information on New South Wales Government legislation, see https://www.legislation.nsw.gov.au.

11. Crown Copyright 2013. Contains public sector information licensed under the Open Government Licence v3.0. https://www.nationalarchives.gov.uk/doc/open-government-licence/version/3/.

12. Copyright © Northern Territory of Australia.

13. Exercise 11 was inspired by a series of exercises in Lee, Hall, and Barone, *American Legal English*, 66–67.

14. *Black's Law Dictionary 12th ed.*, s.v. "burglary."

15. The authors have diligently attempted to ensure that the Criminal Code of Canada sections reproduced in this exercise are accurate. However, they are

reproduced here for educational use only; they do not represent legal advice, nor should they be used as a resource for anyone providing legal advice. Their inclusion here does not represent the endorsement of any government body, and THESE MATERIALS ARE NOT AN OFFICIAL VERSION.

16. Crown Copyright 2007. Contains public sector information licensed under the Open Government Licence v3.0. https://www.nationalarchives.gov.uk/doc/open-government-licence/version/3/.

17. Copyright © Northern Territory of Australia.

## Chapter 2

1. For a general discussion of case law in the context of United States law, see Arthur T. Von Mehren and Peter L. Murray, *Law in the United States* (Cambridge University Press, 2007), 7–13.

2. *Black's Law Dictionary 11th ed.,* s.v. "common law."

3. For a detailed comparison of legal reasoning in common law and civil law, see Konrad Zweigert and Hein Kötz, *Introduction to Comparative Law* (Oxford University Press, 1998), 256–65.

4. The basic concept for this illustration is from Charles R. Calleros, *Legal Method and Writing* (Aspen Publishers, 2002), 52–53.

5. Most of the cases that you will read in this chapter happen to involve statutes. That is simply because, as we explained earlier, the cases that we have chosen skew heavily toward criminal law—an area of law that has largely been codified in the majority of common law jurisdictions. There will be some "pure" common law cases in chapter 3. (See pages 110–120.)

6. People v. Ravenscroft, 198 Cal.App.3d 639, 642–643 (1988).

7. Adapted from James v. United States, 238 F.2d 681 (9th Cir. 1956).

8. Crown Copyright 1972. Contains public sector information licensed under the Open Government Licence v3.0. https://www.nationalarchives.gov.uk/doc/open-government-licence/version/3/.

9. Crown Copyright 1985. Contains public sector information licensed under the Open Government Licence v3.0. https://www.nationalarchives.gov.uk/doc/open-government-licence/version/3/.

10. In New York, unlike in most common law jurisdictions, the term "Supreme Court" refers to a kind of trial court, not to the highest court in the state. "Supreme Court, Civil and Criminal Courts," New York State Unified Court System, accessed March 6, 2023, https://www.nycourts.gov/courts/cts-NYC-Supreme.shtml. "Structure of the Courts," New York State Unified Court System, accessed March 6, 2023, https://www.nycourts.gov/courts/structure.shtml.

## Chapter 3

1. For a more detailed analysis of this process, see Dernbach et al., *A practical guide*, 75–157.

2. Marta Baffy and Kirsten Schaetzel, *Academic Legal Discourse and Analysis: Essential Skills for International Students Studying Law in the United States* (Aspen Publishing, 2019), 263–269.

3. John Hinds, "Reader versus Writer Responsibility: A New Typology," in *Landmark Essays on ESL Writing*, ed. Ulla Connor and Robert B. Kaplan (Reading: Addison-Wesley, 1987), 63–74.

4. The legal authorities and the hypo in exercise 1 were inspired by exercises on writing advice letters in Calleros, *Legal Method*, 493–506.

5. Exercise 2 was inspired by a series of exercises in Lee, Hall, and Barone, *American Legal English*, 112–115. The statutes were developed with reference to Restatement (Third) of Torts: Intentional Torts to Persons § 7 TD (2018), as well as Restatement (Second) of Torts §§ 35, 37, 42, 43, 44, 45, and 120 (1965).

6. The statutes in this exercise are based on the common law definition of burglary and the California definition of theft. See CA Penal Code §§ 486, 487 (2022) and People v. Earle, 222 Cal. App. 2d 476, 477 (Ct. App. 1963).

7. This case was inspired by a hypo in Calleros, *Legal Method*, 77.

8. This hypo is based on In re Roland A., No. F062362, 2011 WL 5560180 (Cal. App. 5th. Nov. 16, 2011).

9. This hypo is loosely based on Cook v. Smith, 33 S.W.3d 548 (Mo. App. 2000).

10. This hypo was inspired by G.L.F. ex rel. Felter v. Heiman, 423 F.Supp.2d 967 (E.D. Mo. 2006).

Below you will find the definitions of some words and phrases that may be useful to you in your legal studies. Most are referred to in other parts of the book, but some are included just because they are important words you should know. A number of them can be used as nouns or verbs (e.g., "appeal"). Note, however, that we have classified and defined them according to how they are used in this book. There may sometimes be alternative legal definitions.

| | |
|---|---|
| Acquit (v.) | To legally free a person accused of a crime |
| Affirm (v.) (US) | To ratify or confirm a former judgment of a court |
| Allege (v.) | To claim or assert that someone has done something illegal or wrong |
| Allow (v.) (UK) | To grant or approve an appeal |
| Appeal (v.) | To make an application to a higher court for a review of a lower court's decision |
| Appellate court (n.) | A court having jurisdiction to hear appeals |
| Application (n.) | A request or petition made to a court or judge |
| Apprehension (n.) | An anxiety or fear that something bad or unpleasant will happen |
| Assault (n.) | A threat or attempt to inflict physical contact or bodily harm on a person |
| Binding (adj.) | Something that is obligatory or required |
| Breach (n.) | Failure to perform an obligation under a contract |
| Burglary (n.) | An illegal entry of (typically) a building with intent to commit a crime |
| Case (n.) | 1. A civil or criminal proceeding before a tribunal, typically a court |
| | 2. An opinion by a court |

| | |
|---|---|
| Case brief (n.) | A summary of a case opinion |
| Charge (with) (v.) | To make a formal statement saying that someone is accused of a crime |
| Civil law (n.) | 1. The system of law that arose in continental Europe, cf. common law |
| | 2. The law regulating the private rights of individuals, cf. criminal law |
| Claim (n.) | A formal assertion of a legal cause of action |
| Clause (n.) | A particular/specific part of a legal document (such as a section, article, or paragraph) |
| Code (n.) | A collection of laws, often covering a defined area |
| Commission (n.) | The act of doing something, e.g., the commission of a crime |
| Common law (n.) | The system of law that developed in England in the pre-modern era and is generally now practiced in English-speaking jurisdictions |
| Compel (v.) | To force or oblige someone to do something |
| Compensation (n.) | Something, typically money, awarded to someone in recognition of loss, suffering, or injury |
| Complainant (n.) | The party who makes the complaint in a legal action or proceeding |
| Complaint (n.) | Typically, the first document filed in court proceedings that sets out the allegations against the defendant; alternatively, any document setting out legal allegations |
| Conditional (adj.) | Subject to one or more conditions or requirements being met |
| Conduct (n.) | The manner in which a person behaves |
| Consent (n.) | Permission for something to happen or agreement to do something |
| Consideration (n.) | The mutual exchange of something of value between the parties to a contract |
| Construe (v.) | To interpret (often a word or phrase in a legal context) in a particular way |
| Contend (v.) | To assert something as a position in an argument |
| Contention (n.) | A point advanced or maintained in a debate or argument |
| Contract (n.) | An agreement between different parties that is enforceable by the court |
| Contravene (v.) | To do something that a law or rule does not allow |

| | |
|---|---|
| Conviction (n.) | A formal declaration by the verdict of a jury or the decision of a judge in a court of law that someone is guilty of a criminal offense |
| Court (n.) | A tribunal in which civil and criminal cases are heard and decided |
| Damages (n.) | A sum of money claimed or awarded in compensation for a loss or an injury |
| Deem (v.) | To consider or judge something in a particular way |
| Defamation (n.) | The law that governs statements that harm the reputation of individuals or entities (for example, companies) |
| Defendant (n.) | A person or group against whom a criminal or civil action is brought |
| Defence (n.) (UK) | |
| Defense (n.) (US) | That which is offered and alleged by a defendant in an action, as a reason in law or fact why the plaintiff/complainant should not recover or establish what he seeks |
| Dismiss (an appeal) (v.) (UK) | To decide, in an appeals court, against an appeal, letting the lower court decision stand |
| Duty of care (n.) | The duty to take proper care to avoid causing some form of foreseeable harm to another |
| Err (v.) | To make a mistake |
| Evidence (n.) | Any object or information that helps to prove or disprove the existence of a fact in issue |
| Facilitate (v.) | To make an action or process easier |
| False imprisonment (n.) | The unlawful restraint and/or imprisonment of a person |
| Felony (n.) | A crime regarded in the United States as more serious than a misdemeanor, typically carrying a minimum sentence of one year in prison |
| Foreseeable (adj.) | Able to be foreseen or predicted |
| Governed (v.) | Determined by or controlled by |
| Hold/holding (v.)/(n.) | To reach a determination or decision about a case/a court's determination of a case |
| Hypo (n.) | A hypothetical factual scenario used to consider and test issues of law |
| Inflict (v.) | To cause something unpleasant or painful to be suffered by someone |

| | |
|---|---|
| Intentionally (adv.) | Done deliberately and on purpose, with awareness of what one is doing |
| IRAC (n.) | A structure for organizing legal writing (Issue, Rule, Application, Conclusion). See chapter 3. |
| Judge (n.) | An official with the authority to decide legal disputes in court |
| Jurisdiction (n.) | The authority or power of the court to determine a dispute between parties; or the territory over which the legal authority of a court extends |
| Jury (n.) | A group of persons chosen to decide on matters of fact in a legal case |
| Kidnap (v.) | To abduct someone and hold them captive, typically to obtain a ransom |
| Larceny (n.) | Theft of personal property |
| Leave of the court (n.) | When a court/judge gives permission to do something not typically allowed by right |
| Liability (n.) | A legal responsibility |
| Material (adj.) | Relevant and significant |
| Misdemeanor (n.) | A crime less serious than a felony |
| Motion (n.) | A formal request to the court made by any party for a desired ruling, order, or judgment |
| Negligence (n.) | A breach of a duty of care that results in harm |
| Objective (adj.) | Something being assessed by reference to what a reasonable person would have known, thought, or done in the same circumstances |
| Offence (n.) (UK) Offense (n.) (US) | An act or omission that constitutes a crime |
| Party (n.) | A natural or legal person involved in legal proceedings or in a contract |
| Perform (v.) | To fulfill obligations under a contract |
| Petition (n.) | A formal written request to a court for an order |
| Proceeding (n.) | Any actions taken before a court so a decision can be made |
| Provision (n.) | A statement of something that must happen or be done within a legal document or in a specific law |
| Prudent (adj.) | Demonstrating a reasonable standard of judgment and caution under the circumstances |
| Quash (v.) | To annul or set aside |
| Reasonable (adj.) | Just, rational, appropriate, and ordinary or usual in the circumstances |

| | |
|---|---|
| Reasonable person (n.) | A person of average caution, care, and consideration showing usual behavior in the circumstances |
| Reckless (adj.) | Knowingly taking an unreasonable and unjustified risk |
| Relief (n.) | Any benefit (e.g., financial compensation, release from a duty, etc.) that an order or judgment of a court can give a party to a lawsuit |
| Reverse (v.) (US) | To make a ruling in an appeal that the judgment of a lower court was incorrect and should therefore be overturned |
| Section (of a statute) (n.) | A part of a written law containing provisions |
| Sentence (n.) | The punishment given to a person convicted of a crime |
| Standing (n.) | The legal capacity for someone to commence or be involved in legal proceedings |
| Stare decisis (n.) | The common law doctrine that decisions made in higher courts bind judges in lower courts, i.e., lower courts must follow the law set out in those decisions when deciding cases of a similar nature |
| Statute (n.) | A written law enacted by a legislature |
| Subject to (v.) | To be conditional or dependent on something |
| Term (n.) | A word or phrase; part of a statute or contract or other legal document containing a provision |
| Terminate (v.) | To bring something to an end |
| Tort (n.) | An act or omission that gives rise to injury or harm to another and constitutes a civil wrong |
| Trespass (v.) | To knowingly enter another owner's property without permission |
| Unauthorized (adj.) | Without legal authority or permission |
| Violate (v.) | To break or disregard a legal obligation |
| Writ (n.) | An order issued by a legal authority with administrative or judicial powers |

*Bibliography*

## Introduction

Kraft, Diane. "Contrastive Analysis and Contrastive Rhetoric in the
Legal Writing Classroom." *New Mexico Law Review* 49, no. 1
(Winter 2019): 35–58.
Ramsfield, Jill. "Is 'Logic' Culturally Based? A Contrastive, International
Approach to the U.S. Law Classroom." *Journal of Legal Education* 47, no. 2
(1997): 157–204.
Spanbauer, Julie. "Lost in Translation in the Law School Classroom:
Assessing Required Coursework in LL.M. Programs for International
Students." *International Journal of Legal Information* 35, no. 3 (2007):
396–446.

## Chapter 1—Reading Statutes

Dernbach, John, Richard Singleton, Cathleen Wharton, Catherine Wasson,
and Joan Ruhtenberg. *A Practical Guide to Legal Writing and Legal
Method*. Aspen Publishing, 2021.
Georgetown Law. *A Guide to Reading, Interpreting and Applying Statutes*.
https://www.law.georgetown.edu/wp-content/uploads/2018/12/A-
Guide-to-Reading-Interpreting-and-Applying-Statutes-1.pdf.
Lee, Debra, Charles Hall, and Susan Barone. *American Legal English: Using
Language in Legal Contexts*, 2nd ed. University of Michigan Press, 2007.
Marmor, Andrei. *The Language of Law*. Oxford University Press, 2014.
Pojanowski, Jeffrey. "Reading Statutes in the Common Law Tradition."
*Virginia Law Review* 101, no. 5 (September 2015): 1357–1424.

## Chapter 2—Reading Cases

Calleros, Charles. *Legal Method and Writing.* Aspen Publishers, 2002.
Garner, Bryan. *Black's Law Dictionary.* Thomson Reuters, 2019.
Von Mehren, Arthur and Peter Murray. *Law in the United States.* Cambridge University Press, 2007.
Zweigert, Konrad and Hein Kötz. *An Introduction to Comparative Law.* Oxford University Press, 1998.

## Chapter 3—Legal Writing—(C)IRAC

Baffy, Marta and Kirsten Schaetzel. *Academic Legal Discourse and Analysis: Essential Skills for International Students Studying Law in the United States.* Aspen Publishing, 2019.
Calleros, Charles. *Legal Method and Writing.* Aspen Publishers, 2002.
Dernbach, John, Richard Singleton, Cathleen Wharton, Catherine Wasson, and Joan Ruhtenberg. *A Practical Guide to Legal Writing and Legal Method.* Aspen Publishing, 2021.
Hinds, John. "Reader Versus Writer Responsibility: A New Typology." in *Landmark Essays on ESL Writing,* edited by Ulla Connor and Robert B. Kaplan, 63–74. Addison-Wesley, 1987.
Lee, Debra, Charles Hall, and Susan Barone. *American Legal English: Using Language in Legal Contexts,* 2nd ed. University of Michigan Press, 2007.

## Further Reading/Useful Sources

Burr, Anne, and Howard Bromberg. *U.S. Legal Practice Skills for International Law Students.* Carolina Academic Press, 2014.
Edwards, Linda. *Legal Writing and Analysis.* Wolters Kluwer Law & Business, 2011.
Garner, Bryan. *Legal Writing in Plain English.* University of Chicago Press, 2001.
Garner, Bryan. *The Elements of Legal Style.* Oxford University Press, 2002.
Haigh, Rupert. *Legal English.* Routledge, 2018.
Johns, Margaret. *Professional Writing for Lawyers.* Carolina Academic Press, 1998.
Krois-Linder, Amy, Matt Firth, and TransLegal. *Introduction to International Legal English.* Cambridge University Press, 2008.

Krois-Linder, Amy and TransLegal. *International Legal English*. Cambridge University Press, 2006.

Lee, Debra, Charles Hall, and Susan Barone. *American Legal English: Using Language in Legal Contexts*, 2nd ed. University of Michigan Press, 2007.

Lundquist, Karen. *Legal Writing and Legal Skills for Foreign LL. M. Students: ESL Workbook*. West Academic Publishing, 2017.

Mason, Catherine. *The Lawyer's English Language Coursebook*. Global English Ltd., 2014.

McGregor, Deborah and Cynthia Adams. *The International Lawyer's Guide to Legal Analysis and Communication in the United States*. Wolters Kluwer, 2008.

Nedzel, Nadia. *Legal Reasoning, Research, and Writing for International Graduate Students*. Wolters Kluwer, 2012.

Reinhart, Susan. *Strategies for Legal Case Reading and Vocabulary Development*. University of Michigan Press, 2007.

Roche, Marc. *Master Legal Vocabulary and Terminology*. IDM Business and Law, 2018.

Thornton, John. *U.S. Legal Reasoning, Writing, and Practice for International Lawyers*. Carolina Academic Press, 2014.

Trachtman, Joel. *The Tools of Argument. How the Best Lawyers Think, Argue, and Win*. CreateSpace, 2013.

Walenn, Jeremy. *English for Law in Higher Education Studies*. Garnet Education, 2009.

Wydick, Richard. *Plain English for Lawyers*. Carolina Academic Press, 2005.

# Answer Keys

## Chapter 1

### Exercise 1

1. c   2. c   3. a   4. b

*Short-answer questions*
1. It provides a definition of who is subject to the statute.
2. No, they would have to show either (a) plus (c) or (b) plus (c). The words "and" and "or" help us decide this.
3. Since there is an obligation under section 3629 to make sure everyone proves their age, there are no circumstances where you could argue that you did not reasonably know the individual was under 21 for the purposes of section 3630(b).

*Suggested answers to hypos*
1. Probably yes. Elements (b) and (c) of Collody Civil Code section 3630 are satisfied here. Under section 3630(b), a person can recover damages from a server only if they "knew, or reasonably should have known, that the person served was under 21." The bartender in this case may not have known that Bob was under 21 (because he looked older), but he "reasonably should have known" because he was required by Collody Civil Code section 3629 to ask Bob for his ID. In addition, section 3630(c) is satisfied because the crash was a foreseeable result of the bartender serving alcohol to a minor.
2. Probably not. As in the previous case, section 3630(b) is satisfied because the waiter "reasonably should have known" Laura was under 21. However, section 3630(c) is probably not satisfied because an allergic reaction to mango was not a foreseeable result of her negligence.

## Exercise 2

*Short-answer questions*

1. "Consumer" means an individual acting for purposes that are wholly or mainly outside that individual's trade, business, craft, or profession.
2. Section 3(2).
3. It implies in every contract a term that the goods will be satisfactory.
4. It uses punctuation to list the factors and uses the word "and" in section 9(2)(b).
5. Just one of them. It uses punctuation to list the circumstances and uses the word "or" in section 9(4)(b).

*True / false questions*

1. F    2. T    3. T    4. F    5. T

*Short-answer questions*

1. A cheap kettle would not be expected to last for a very long time, so you may have less chance of using the statute to make a claim than if you had bought a very expensive kettle that broke after three years.
2. Since you knew there was a defect, you may have difficulty making a claim under the statute because of subsection (4), but it may depend on the facts and what other information you were given about the product.
3. Subsection (6) means that you can take account of information given in advertisements for a product. On these facts, there seems to be a clear implication from the advertisement that you could play the game in the picture on that laptop. Therefore, it would appear likely you could claim the laptop was "unsatisfactory" under subsection (1).

## Exercise 3

*Word-matching exercise*

1. d    2. e    3. f    4. a    5. c    6. g    7. b

*True / false questions*

1. T    2. F    3. T    4. F

*Multiple-choice questions*

1. d    2. b    3. a

*Short-answer questions*
1. Yes, Brad told a lie to the enforcement officer that he had instructed Dawn not to sell any tobacco or vaping products at the shop. This contravenes section 3(4)(b).
2. The bookstore, as owner of the space in which the coffee shop is located, could be liable under section 2.1(2). It is possible that the college, as owners of the building, could also be liable.
3. The bookstore may have a defense under section 2.1(3) if it can show it exercised reasonable care and diligence to prevent the contravention.
4. Brad may be able to rely on a defense under section 2.1(3) by demonstrating that he had exercised reasonable care and diligence to prevent the contravention.


## Exercise 4

*Gap-fill exercise*
1. guardian
2. parental responsibility; custody
3. provisions

*Short-answer questions*
1. No, they would just need one section to be applicable to them. The use of "or" in the list indicates this.
2. Yes, since the statute explicitly states, "the consent of <u>each</u> of the following."
3. Reasonable would be doing everything a normal person in those circumstances would do. The means of communication would be relevant (e.g., was it a call to a number or message to an email account that was known to be generally used); how much time was given for a response to the message; when the message was sent/left.

*True / false questions*
1. F    2. T    3. T    4. F    5. T

*Multiple-choice questions*
1. d    2. b    3. a

## Exercise 5

*Gap-fill exercise*

abducted, ransom, compel, constitutes, felony, confined, inflict, hostage, flight, reward

*Suggested answers to hypos*

1.  The Washington statutes require an "abduction," and in ordinary English, that word means taking someone from one place to another against their will. Assuming this meaning of the word (and remember, this may not be the way it is actually defined in Washington law—there may be case law on this point), it looks like the two men abducted the employees when they marched them back to the storeroom. Since the most likely explanation of their action is that they wanted to keep the employees from alerting anyone about the robbery while they were getting away, they would be guilty of first-degree kidnapping under RCW 9A.40.020 (1)(b).

    Although the first man admits that he is holding the cashier as a shield or hostage as required by (1)(a), this is before he "abducts" him.

    The robbers are guilty of second-degree kidnapping in Oregon under ORS 163.225(1)(a) when they march the employees to the storeroom, because they take them from one place to another with the intent to interfere with their liberty. (They are probably not guilty under (1)(b) because the police are almost certain to find them in the storeroom.) The real question is whether they are guilty of first-degree kidnapping. You could argue that they are being kept as "shields" because the robbers are holding them in order to protect themselves while they escape, which might satisfy ORS 163.235 (1)(b).

2.  The first question under the Washington statutes is whether the supervisor has abducted the janitor. Although he does not use force, he does trick her into going with him, unseen, to an undisclosed location. This is probably enough. If it is, he could be guilty of first-degree kidnapping under RCW 9A.40.020(1)(b) because in fooling the janitor into working for him without pay, he is almost certainly committing a felony. It is even possible that (1)(a) is satisfied, if the janitor's unpaid labor is considered a "reward."

    The supervisor also satisfies the requirement of ORS 163.225(1)(a) of taking someone from one place to another. There could be a question of consent, but given his dishonesty and her disability, it seems unlikely that a court would find she consented. He may have also satisfied (1)(b). Here, although he has clearly taken her to a place where she is unlikely to be found, there is a question of whether she is "confined" there, as he is using no force to keep her there. One could argue, however, that she is confined both by the remote location and by his deception.

The question of first-degree kidnapping is more complicated. It is not clear that any of the four purposes listed in ORS 163.235(1) fits this situation perfectly. One could argue that she is being forced to deliver property (her labor) to him, which would satisfy (1)(a), though it isn't clear that this is being delivered as a "ransom." It isn't obviously clear that she is being held as a "hostage" or that she is being "terrorized" either. Whether any of these conditions are satisfied would have to be determined based on further legal research.

3. Again, the first question under the Washington statutes is whether the bookkeeper has been abducted. The problem is that he was not coerced or forced to go on the trip, and may even have been happy to go. If there has been an abduction, then the executive has almost certainly committed first-degree kidnapping, because her purpose for taking him away from the business was to facilitate a felony. If not, then she wouldn't be guilty of second-degree kidnapping, either.

   The first question under ORS 163.225 is whether the bookkeeper has been taken on the cruise with the "intent to interfere substantially" with his "personal liberty." One could argue that this means intending to do something that keeps a person from going where they want to go, and that the executive intended to prevent the bookkeeper from going to the office—which is where he would have wanted to go had he known what was going on.

   As in hypo 2, it is unclear whether any of the four purposes listed in ORS 163.235 (1) fits this situation.

4. One could argue that the father is guilty of first-degree kidnapping under RCW 9A.40.020(1)(e) because he took his daughter to another state to "interfere with the performance of [a] governmental function," namely the court's judgments about the daughter's school and the mother's custody of her.

   If the father is not guilty of first-degree kidnapping because interference with a government function is not interpreted this way in Washington, he may also not be guilty of second-degree kidnapping because he meets the requirements of the defense outlined in RCW 9A.40.030(2).

   Under Oregon law, the father is probably not guilty of kidnapping at all because ORS 163.235 does not appear to be applicable, and the elements of the defense outlined in ORS 163.225(2) are all satisfied.

Exercise 6

*True / false questions*
1. T    2. F    3. T    4. F

*Suggested answers to hypos*
1.  You had lawful authority to have and use the bank card, so you could not have had the intention of committing an indictable offense. Therefore, you could not be guilty of an offense under section 192J or 192K.
2.  Ordering something knowing that you probably cannot pay your friend back is likely to be theft or fraud. Therefore, you would most likely be guilty under section 192J, and also even 192K, of dealing and possessing identification information with the intention of committing an offense.
3.  While using a fake ID may be a crime, under section 192M(1), Part 4AB does not apply to a person dealing with their own identification information. Therefore, Fred could not be guilty under the Act.

Exercise 7

*Word-matching exercise*
1. d    2. a    3. g    4. f    5. h    6. e    7. c    8. b

*Short-answer questions*
1.  27.1(1)
2.  27.1(2)
3.  77 (a) and (g)
4.  77 (b) and (f)

*Answers to hypos*
1.  The criminal code of Canada applies here because the incident occurs on an aircraft that is either in Canadian airspace or is outside Canadian airspace but on an aircraft registered in Canada (Criminal Code of Canada, section 27.1(2)). Oscar could most likely be charged under section 77(a) of the Criminal Code of Canada—committing an act of violence against a person that is likely to endanger the safety of the aircraft. He could also possibly be charged with hijacking under section 77(d) because the aircraft had to change its flight plan.
2.  The first question would be whether the Criminal Code of Canada applies (Criminal Code of Canada, section 27.1(2)). If the incident occurred outside Canadian airspace, it would depend on whether the

aircraft was registered in Canada. Assuming it does apply, the most relevant offense for which Peggy could be charged is section 77(c)—causing damage to an aircraft in service that renders the aircraft incapable of flight or that is likely to endanger the safety of the aircraft in flight. However, this might not be successful because it is arguable no material damage was caused that would endanger the safety of the aircraft in flight. She might also be charged with section 77(a), if a rough push of the air steward could be said to be an act of violence endangering the safety of the aircraft.

3.    The airline or crew members could defend themselves against an action brought by Oscar using section 27.1(1), which allows them to use any force necessary to prevent a serious injury to the air steward that Oscar attacked.

4.    The crew could defend themselves using section 27.1(1), though they would have to show that her actions were likely to cause immediate and serious injury to the aircraft or to any person or property in it.

## Exercise 8

*Multiple-choice questions*
1. c    2. c

*True / false questions*
1. F    2. T    3. F    4. T    5. T

*Short-answer questions*
1.    An example could include a situation where a person accepts the offer of a bottle of normal-strength beer, without knowing that it contains a very strong drug that would cause the person to feel very drunk and not in control of themselves.

2.    Barry has caused Jane to become intoxicated for the purposes of section 38A(2). Although Jane knows she is consuming strong alcohol and her senses may already be slightly impaired from having drunk beer earlier in the evening, she does not know that the shot also contains a strong drug, so Barry's actions would be caught by 38A(2)(a)(i). It is highly likely she would object to the level of impairment, so the situation is covered by the definition of "harm" under section 38A(1). Barry prepared the drink by adding the drug for the purposes of 38A(3). Therefore, Barry is likely to be guilty of an offense under section 38A of the Act.

3.  All the other team members consumed the brownies not knowing they contained marijuana, and so, on the face of it, Sarah may be liable under section 38A(2)(a)(i). However, section 38A(4) may help Sarah if she can show that she reasonably thought the other teammates would not have objected to the drug being added to the brownies. The words used in the invitation, the fact that the team had been drinking heavily all night, and any other patterns of behavior shown by the team on previous occasions may provide grounds for Sarah to rely on this section. In that case, she would not be guilty of an offense under the Act. Alternatively, she may try to argue that she did not intend to harm her teammates under section 38A(2)(b), although the arguments would be the same as for a defense using 38A(4).

## Exercise 9

*True / false questions*
1. T    2. F    3. F

*Short-answer questions*
1.  A body that trades for profit; imputation.
2.  It would need to show serious financial loss. In other words, it would have to prove that it lost a lot of money because of the statement, which may be difficult because there could be lots of reasons for the loss.
3.  You need to show that the statement is substantially true (not necessarily 100% true in every respect). The meaning of "substantially" is open to interpretation. Moreover, where more than one statement/claim has been made (defined as "imputation"), even if one of the statements cannot be said to be substantially true, the claimant has to show their reputation has been seriously harmed. This, again, is a matter for interpretation.
4.  Website operators have a defense if they can show that they did not post a statement themselves.
5.  To defeat this defense, a claimant needs to show three things: that the claimant could not determine who posted the statement (e.g., if it was posted anonymously), that the claimant asked the operator to take it down, and that the operator did not do so "in accordance with any provision contained in regulations." (Note that 5(3)c refers to regulations that are not included here. Applying this subsection would therefore require more research on your part.)

*Suggested answer to short paragraph*

You can probably rely on truth as a defense. Moreover, the claimants probably cannot show serious damage to reputation (in the case of the chairman) or serious financial loss (in the case of the company). The website is probably also not liable. Under section 2(1), you can claim that what you wrote was substantially true. Some of the details were incorrect, but they do not affect the force of what you wrote. Moreover, the company's sales are not affected, so they could not claim damages because they have not suffered serious financial loss as required by section 1(2). The chairman likewise may find it difficult to make a claim because, even if some of the details were not 100% accurate, the inaccurate details do not on their own cause serious harm to his reputation. The website is probably protected by section 5(2) because it did not post the statements and they were not made anonymously, but rather in your name.

## Exercise 10

*Gap-fill exercise*
1. tail docked
2. declawed
3. horse firing
4. ears cropped

*Multiple-choice questions (group 1)*
1. d   2. a   3. b

*True / false questions*
1. F   2. T   3. T   4. F   5. T

*Multiple-choice questions (group 2)*
1. c   2. b   3. a

*Short-answer questions*
1. Under section 24(1), while you may not intend to hurt an animal or cause it harm, you can still be liable if you act recklessly. In other words, you do something stupid or without enough care, and it results in harm to an animal. For example, if you drive with your car window open to allow your dog to put its head in the wind and it is hit, you could be said to have acted recklessly.
2. Yes, under section 24(7), it is an offense to dock a dog's tail unless a vet does it for the health of the animal concerned. Cutting the tail just for cosmetic reasons would not be acceptable under the Act.

## Exercise 11

*Lead-in questions*
1. No.
2. It was a way of differentiating burglary from theft, making it a more serious offense.
3. Committing a crime at night is arguably more serious (people are more likely to be home; there is less chance of detection, etc.).
4. It simplifies the offense, and in modern times, the breaking and night requirements are not as relevant as before.

*Multiple-choice questions*
1. c   2. d   3. b   4. b

*Short-answer questions*
1. Entering a home during the day with the intent to commit a theft inside.
2. Maine, Louisiana, United Kingdom.
3. Louisiana.
4. Someone visits a party as an invited guest. While there, they notice an expensive antique that does not seem to be secured. They decide to hide until after the party finishes and the guests go home in order to steal it.
5. Louisiana, maybe Maine if a car can be said to be a "structure."
6. Louisiana, probably Maine and United Kingdom.
7. Probably none.
8. Maine.
9. United Kingdom.

## Exercise 12

*Word-matching exercise*
1. e   2. c   3. a   4. b   5. f   6. d

*True / false questions*
1. F   2. T   3. F   4. F   5. F   6. T   7. F

*Short-answer questions*
1. The managing director and the company both have health and safety duties to employees of the company. By having a detailed written health and safety policy, it may be argued that the company fulfilled its duties to workers but that the managing director, through his instructions to all site foremen, has breached his duty by ordering that old harnesses should not be replaced (though the claimant may also seek to argue that the boss

was acting as the company in his instructions). This was the principal cause of the accident. However, since Bob was not killed but only injured, the UK and Australian Acts cannot apply. The situation would probably be caught by the Canadian statute, which requires just harm, not death, for liability to be established.

2.  Arguably under all the statutes, Pat's employer has breached a duty of care owed to her by turning a blind eye to her breaches of regulations. It has also resulted in her death, which means all the statutes could apply. The company may argue that they fulfilled their duty by warning Pat to be more careful of the regulations, though if she repeatedly ignores them, the company would probably need to show some sort of disciplinary action or intervention was conducted into her actions. If this defense was unsuccessful, it is likely on the face of it that the company would be liable under all three statutes. However, in addition, under the UK and Australian statutes, the breach must be a "substantial" contributor or element to the accident. The company may seek to argue that her consumption of alcohol was the most important factor in the accident and that any breaches by the company were not sufficiently substantial to make them liable.

## Exercise 13

*Word-matching exercise*
1. j   2. k   3. d   4. g   5. b   6. c   7. e   8. a   9. h   10. f   11. i

*Multiple-choice questions*
1. c   2. d   3. a   4. b

*Short-answer questions*
1.  New Jersey and North Carolina.
2.  No.
3.  No. A.R.S. § 25-112(C) prohibits Arizona residents from getting married in another state in order to get around Arizona marriage laws.
4.  New Jersey does not restrict cousin marriage at all, so it should be valid there. It would not be allowed in North Carolina because they are double first cousins.
5.  The marriage could not be declared void after the death of either of the spouses, assuming that they had lived together and had a child together.
6.  It would be legal in New Jersey and North Carolina, of course, since those states allow cousin marriages generally. It would also be legal in Wisconsin because the woman is more than 55 years old. It would be

legal in Maine with a physician's certificate of genetic counseling, and in Arizona if either person can prove that they cannot reproduce.

7. They could get a physician's certificate of genetic counseling.

8. Both states generally prohibit marriages between first cousins, and both prohibit residents from getting married in other states to evade these prohibitions. However, both states also have exceptions that allow cousins to marry. In Maine, it would probably be acceptable for any cousins to get married in a state like New Jersey, as long as they get a physician's certificate of genetic counseling. Arizona, however, would only accept a such a marriage between cousins who are either 65 or older, or if one person could prove that they could not reproduce.

## Chapter 2

### Exercise 1

*Word-matching exercise*
1. d   2. f   3. e   4. c   5. b   6. a   7. g

*Gap-fill exercise*
1. affirmed
2. appellant
3. dismissed
4. held
5. allowed
6. reversed
7. appealed

### Exercise 2

*Gap-fill exercise*
1. penal
2. maliciously
3. acts
4. real
5. vandalism
6. defaces
7. graffiti

*Matching exercise*

1. c   2. d   3. f   4. e   5. a   6. b

*Short-answer questions*
1.  California Court of Appeal.
2.  Nicholas Y. was found guilty of vandalism by the trial court.
3.  Nicholas Y.
4.  The marks he had written could be easily removed, so he had not defaced the glass for the purposes of the statute.
5.  No.
6.  No.
7.  Yes.
8.  The word "deface."
9.  In *MacKinney*, the defendant was acquitted for writing on a sidewalk with chalk, so the facts could be said to be similar.
10. Nicholas Y. wants to use *Mackinney* to try to argue that his case was similar and that a mark that could be easily removed could not be "defacing."
11. Because the statute on vandalism had been amended, so the decision in *MacKinney* was no longer relevant.
12. The court held that an easily removable mark was still defacing for the statute. It noted that the plain meaning of the word "deface" does not include the idea of "permanence." Moreover, it also reasoned that marks made on any surfaces must be removed to restore them to their original condition, so it would be irrational to say that marks on only some surfaces are graffiti. It would not make sense to say some marks are graffiti and some are not, based on how hard they are to remove.

## Exercise 3

*Word-matching exercise*
1. d   2. c   3. a   4. b

*Multiple-choice questions*
1. a   2. d   3. a

## Exercise 4

*Short-answer/multiple-choice questions*
1.  Burglary is generally defined as an unauthorized entry into a building or some sort of structure with the intention of committing a crime. Entering

a home intending to rape someone would therefore come within most burglary statutes.

2.  Probably you would not, as long as you could say that you reasonably believed you were being invited in.

3.  a.

4.  d.

*True/false*

1. T    2. T    3. F    4. F    5. T

*Multiple-choice questions*

1.  a.

2.  b.

## Exercise 5

*Word-matching exercise*

1. d    2. a    3. c    4. b

*Short-answer questions*

1.  The defendant was convicted of two offenses of burglary in the Crown Court.

2.  The defendant, Brown.

3.  He had observed the top half of Brown's body reaching inside a shop through a broken window.

4.  Because Parkin was acquitted of larceny when found with one arm inside a building as the court found he was not in the building for the purposes of the statute.

5.  Because the statute had been amended since that case, so the words relied upon in the *Parkin* case no longer formed part of the law.

6.  Whether a defendant needs to be wholly inside a building to be a trespasser for the purposes of section 9(1) of the Theft Act 1968.

7.  The court believed that it would be a ridiculous proposition that a person can go along the street, break a shop window, put his hand within and steal goods, and not be held to have entered the shop as a trespasser. Therefore, breaking a window and putting a hand, arm, or upper part of a body through it was capable of being found to be an entry for the purposes of the Theft Act 1968.

## Exercise 6

*Word-matching exercise*
1. a   2. d   3. e   4. h   5. g   6. f   7. b   8. c

*Gap-fill exercise*
1. contention
2. well settled
3. governed
4. relief

*True / false questions*
1. F   2. T   3. T   4. F

*Short-answer questions*
1. When someone has been detained unlawfully and seeks immediate release.
2. No, the court denied the petition as it is a condition of writs of habeas corpus that the subject of the petition should be eligible for immediate release. In this case, release was not sought by the petitioner but simply a move to a more appropriate facility.
3. This decision is likely to have been the same, for the same reasons in 2. above.
4. They were trying to raise awareness of what they believed was poor treatment of animals, linking what would generally be termed "person rights" to the rights of all living things. They may also have been seeking a ruling or comment by the court that the primate in question could be legally defined as a person, though presumably they would not have expected to be successful.

## Exercise 7

*Case brief for* People v. Toomes

Name and citation
People v. Toomes 148 Cal.App.2d 465 (1957)

Procedural history
The People, Plaintiff and Appellant, John H. TOOMES and Philander Smith, Defendants and Respondents. California Court of Appeal, 1957. Toomes and

Smith were accused of burglarizing a locked car under PC section 459. They were committed for trial at the preliminary hearing. They made a motion to set aside the information (PC section 995.) Motion granted. People appeal. Reversed.

Facts
All the doors and the trunk of a car were locked. Defendants forced open the trunk and stole the spare tire.

Issue
Was the locked trunk a "door" for purposes of Penal Code section 459?

Holding
Yes, a trunk counts as a door under the statute.

Reasoning
If we look at the dictionary for the ordinary, everyday English meaning of "door," we see that it can be applied to a trunk. The purpose of the statute is to make it a more serious crime to break into a locked vehicle than just to take something from an unlocked vehicle. This purpose would be defeated if a trunk—a lockable compartment often used for carrying valuable things—was not defined as a door.

*Case brief for* People v. Malcolm
Name and citation
People v. Malcolm 47 Cal.App.3d 217 (1975)

Procedural history
The People of the State of California, Plaintiff and Appellant v. Claude William Malcolm, Defendant and Respondent. The defendant was accused of violating California Penal Code section 459, burglary of a locked automobile. The defense made a motion to dismiss the charge on the basis that the car was not locked at the time of the offense. The motion was granted. The People appealed from the dismissal. Dismissal reversed.

Facts
Armstrong parked his car and locked all the doors with a key. The windows were rolled up and closed. However, the lock on one wind wing was broken so it couldn't be locked. The defendant and his friends later came across Armstrong's car, and one of them put his hand through the wind wing and

opened the door. Some officers who had been secretly observing them saw them take property from the car and arrested them.

## Issue
Were the doors of the vehicle "locked" for the purposes of section 459 when one of the windows could not be fully secured?

## Holding
The doors were locked and, therefore, auto burglary was established for the purposes of section 459.

## Reasoning
In *People v. Toomes*, the Court held that the cover of a car trunk was a door for the purposes of the relevant provision of the statute. In coming to its judgment, the Court considered that legislators had sought to prevent the breaking into of the interior sections of locked cars. In this case, the Court concluded the significance of *Toomes* was that common sense must be used in interpreting Penal Code section 459. The Court was convinced that the auto burglary statute should be construed flexibly with the principal objective of discouraging the social evil that statute was designed to prevent.

*Case brief for* In re Lamont R.
### Name and citation
In re Lamont R., 245 Cal.Rptr. 870 (1988)

### Procedural history
The People, Plaintiff and Respondent, v. Lamont R., Defendant and Appellant. California Court of Appeal. Lamont R. was charged with attempted vehicular burglary. The court denied a motion to dismiss for insufficient evidence and found the allegations to be true beyond a reasonable doubt. Defendant appealed from the findings and disposition order. Reversed.

### Summary of the facts
A police officer arrived at the scene where a truck had been broken into. Unable to reuse the original lock that had previously secured the truck, he closed the doors of the truck and wrapped two chains round each other and hooked them to the opposite sides of the doors. Later, appellant and a companion approached the truck and unhooked the chains, opening one of the doors of the truck. They were then arrested.

Legal Issue

The issue is whether the trailer was locked within the meaning of section 459 of the California Penal Code by chains wrapped around the hook of a door.

Holding

The doors were not locked for the purposes of section 459.

Reasoning

The legislature clearly intended the statute to make it a more serious crime to break into a locked vehicle than an unlocked one. *People v. Malcolm* can be distinguished from this case because in *Malcolm*, the perpetrator had to push a window open, reach in, and unlock the doors. In this case, the defendant used no pressure and did not disengage any lock. If the truck was considered locked in this case, any car door or trunk without a functioning lock would be deemed "locked" merely by the owner's act of closing it. The attorney general has argued that "locked" should be construed to mean "secured insofar as possible." This would be inconsistent with the legislature's intent that unauthorized entry into a locked vehicle should be a more serious crime than unauthorized entry into one that is not locked.

# Chapter 3

We include a number of sample or suggested possible IRAC answers to some of the hypos in the texts, for your information. We do not include an answer for every hypo, and there may be different ways to answer the questions correctly.

## Exercise 1

*Gap-fill exercise*
1. term
2. perform
3. party, terminate
4. breach
5. vandalism
6. material

*True / false questions*
1. F   2. F   3. T   4. T

*Short-answer questions*

1.  If the breach is not material, section 9(1) states that the non-breaching party is not able to terminate. Therefore, if the non-breaching party terminates, they would have breached the contract itself and be potentially liable for damages under section 8(2). The relevant case is *Bob's Builders v. Ralph*, 8 Cdy. 987 (2004).

2.  It may depend on how much lower the quality was of the balls that were supplied. If they were not of significantly lower quality, termination may not be available. However, the answer to this question is not 100% clear from the case law.

*Sample answer using CRAC form*

Fred may not fire Wally because, although he breached the contract by ignoring the term specifying the use of Colorama paint, his breach was not material. A breach may be material under Collody Civil Code section 9(2)a. if it "deprives the non-breaching party of the benefit that the contract is supposed to provide." Section 9(3) states that if the breach is not material, the breaching party must be allowed to perform the contract. In *Ali's v. Holmes*, the court of appeal explained that a party can be deprived of the benefit that the contract is supposed to provide if the party receives "something substantially different" from what the contract specified. In that case, a sporting goods store had a contract for basketballs, but received volleyballs instead. Since it is very unlikely that a customer who enters a store looking for a basketball would be willing to buy a volleyball, the store had clearly received something substantially different from what it had contracted for. By contrast, Fred received something substantially similar to what he had contracted for when Wally did the job with another brand of paint that was just as good as the one that the contract specified. In fact, whatever injury Fred suffered was arguably less than that suffered in another case where the court held that the breach was not material. In *Bob's Builders v. Ralph*, Ralph, a subcontractor, was three hours late with concrete for Bob's building project, and Bob's fired them. Even though this breach could have had some genuine impact on the project, the court still decided that it was not serious enough to be material, and that Bob's had actually breached the contract by firing them for a minor breach. In sum, because Wally's breach was not material, Fred may not fire him without breaching the contract himself.

## Exercise 2

*Word-matching exercise*
1. b     2. c     3. a     4. d

*True / false questions*
1. F     2. T     3. F     4. T

*Multiple-choice questions*
1. c     2. a

*Sample answer using IRAC form*
The issue is whether the store manager and security guard had probable cause to detain Barbara as soon as she put the shampoo in her own shopping bag. Under Collody Civil Code section 233, a merchant may detain someone for a reasonable time to investigate whether that person is trying to take goods without paying for them, and they cannot be held liable for this so long as they have probable cause to do so. Barbara may argue that there was no probable cause because her case is like *Rock's v. Disco*. In *Rock's*, a man in a clothing store put a wallet into his pocket and was immediately detained. He claimed that he was merely trying to see if it was comfortable. The court held that the fact that the man had put the wallet where store workers could not see it was not, by itself, enough for probable cause—especially because it should have occurred to them that there could be a reasonable explanation for his behavior. Similarly, Barbara can argue that all she did was to put the shampoo where it could not be seen, and that the manager should have waited for more evidence before detaining her. She will have more trouble, however, arguing that there was an obvious innocent explanation for what she was doing. Stores provide shopping baskets and carts for their customers for a reason—so that they can carry the goods that they might want to buy around the shop while keeping them in view of the people who work there. In fact, what Barbara did is arguably more like what the customer did in *Mustard v. Mayo*—a case where the court did find probable cause. In *Mustard*, a customer in a bookshop put a magazine under his jacket and was blocked when he headed for the door. The court distinguished *Rock's* by noting that there was no obvious innocent explanation for this behavior. Here, Paymore can argue that, even if Barbara really did not intend to steal the shampoo, she certainly acted as though she was going to do so. Although there are good arguments on both sides, because there was no reasonable explanation for her behavior that

would have been obvious to store employees, if Barbara sues Paymore for false imprisonment, she will probably lose.

## Exercise 3

*Short-answer questions*
1. Felony.
2. Misdemeanor.
3. Intent.

*True / false questions*
1. T    2. F    3. T

*Short-answer questions*
1. They have clarified that a home is somewhere where you generally live. The court will look at how often you live there and for how long you have done so.
2. You must (1) intentionally take someone else's property (2) without permission (3) with the intent to keep it.
3. It found that the defendant did not intend to take someone else's property because he (rightfully) believed it was his.

*Sample answer using CRAC form*
Robert is not guilty of burglary because he did not intend to commit a felony when he broke into David's car. To be guilty of burglary under Collody Penal Code section 45, a person must break into someone's home, at night, with the intent to commit a felony inside. Stealing something worth more than $200 is grand theft, which is a felony under Collody law. In this case, however, Robert did not intend to commit grand theft because he intended to take back a painting that he thought was rightfully his. In fact, this case is much like *People v. Flint*, in which a person broke into his neighbor's home to take back his TV. The only difference is that in this case, Robert was mistaken about owning the painting, whereas the defendant in *Flint* was not. However, since this difference is irrelevant to the question of Robert's intent, *Flint* should still apply. In conclusion, because Robert did not intend to commit a felony, he is not guilty of burglary.

(Note that it is not strictly necessary to discuss whether you thought David's car was a home under Collody law because it would not change the answer to the hypo. However, an answer that does discuss this issue should probably take the point of view that David's car is his home because he does not have anywhere else to live. Although one could argue that he does not solely live in the car because he sometimes stays at Antonio's house and uses his water for showers and to clean his clothes, that is probably not enough to show that he lives at his friend's house. In fact, because of its lack of shower and laundry facilities, David's car is probably pretty similar to the tent that the court of appeal found to be a home in *People v. Slate*.)

## Exercise 5

*True / false questions*
1. F    2. T    3. T    4. F    5. F

*Gap-fill exercise*
1.  apprehension
2.  threaten
3.  unambiguous
4.  imminent
5.  objective
6.  conditional

*Sample answer using CIRAC form*
It is likely that Andrew would be convicted of assault under s.22.01(a)(2) in these circumstances. The issue is whether a reasonable person under the circumstances would consider Andrew's words and conduct to be an objective threat of imminent bodily injury for the purposes of the statute. Under s.22.01(a)(2) of the Texas Penal Code, assault is defined as when a person intentionally or knowingly threatens another with imminent bodily injury. A conditional threat can still be considered imminent, such as brandishing a gun and threatening to kill a person if they did not go away, even if there was no intention to actually inflict what was threatened (*Tidwell v. State*, 187 S.W.3d 773508 S.W.3d 766 (2006)). However, ambiguous and vague threats have been found not to constitute assault (*Jones v. Shipley*, 507 S.W.3d 756 (2016)). Moreover, physically poking someone in the chest three or four times has likewise been held not to constitute assault by threat of imminent bodily injury (*Moore v. City of Wylie*, 319 S.W.3d 778 (2010)). In this case, even though Andrew may not have intended to actually strike the youth(s) with the baseball bat, his words and conduct taken together are not really ambiguous or vague. Even though conditional, a reasonable person would conclude

that there was an imminent threat of bodily injury if a baseball bat was being waved with the words used. The situation is much closer to the *Tidwell* case than the other cases referred to above. It goes beyond merely poking in the chest or making a vague or ambiguous threat of possible actions. In conclusion, in such circumstances, it is likely Andrew would be found guilty of assault under s.22.01(a)(2) of the Texas Penal Code.

## Exercise 6

*Word-matching exercise*
1. f    2. e    3. b    4. c    5. d    6. a

*Gap-fill exercise*
1.  directed verdict
2.  proximate cause
3.  remand
4.  gives rise to
5.  dispositive
6.  foreseeable